ANOTHER GREAT

'I hope one day to meet the demented g[...]
Dyer aboard an American aircraft carrier. The result sounds in places as if
Sterne en route to his sentimental journey had paused for a week's stint on
HMS Victory . . . In the end one is forced to call it "a Dyer book," which
luckily for him and us is a high compliment' **John Jeremiah Sullivan**

'No writer can flex and stretch in digressive prose more congenially than
Dyer' *Sunday Telegraph*

'Geoff Dyer has managed to do again what he does best: insert himself
into an exotic and demanding environment (sometimes, his own flat, but
here, the violent wonders of an aircraft carrier) and file a report that mixes
empathetic appreciation with dips into brilliant comic deflation. Welcome
aboard the edifying and sometimes hilarious ship Dyer' **Billy Collins**

'Shrewd, funny, original . . . very good company on the page'
Andrew Motion, *Guardian*

'A great day is any day you get to read Geoff Dyer, and this book is no
exception. Witty, empathetic, and insatiably curious, Dyer is the perfect
guide to [this] floating world' **Sam Lipsyte**

'Geoff Dyer delights in producing books that are unique, like keys'
New Yorker

Also by Geoff Dyer

Zona

Working the Room: Essays and Reviews 1999–2010

Jeff in Venice, Death in Varanasi

The Ongoing Moment

Yoga for People Who Can't Be Bothered to Do It

*Anglo-English Attitudes: Essays, Reviews
and Misadventures 1984–99*

Paris Trance

Out of Sheer Rage

The Missing of the Somme

The Search

But Beautiful

The Colour of Memory

Ways of Telling: The Work of John Berger

ANOTHER GREAT DAY AT SEA

Life Aboard the USS *George H.W. Bush*

GEOFF DYER

With Photographs by Chris Steele-Perkins

CANONGATE

Edinburgh · London

This edition published in Great Britain in 2015
by Canongate Books Ltd,
14 High Street, Edinburgh, EH1 1TE

www.canongate.tv

Published in the United States by
Pantheon Books, a division of Random House LLC, New York,
and in Canada by Random House of Canada Limited, Toronto,
Penguin Random House companies.
Simultaneously, first published in Great Britain by
Visual Editions, London.

This work is part of a series entitled Writers in Residence.

British Library Cataloging-in-Publication Data

A catalogue record of this book is available on request
from the British Library

ISBN 978 1 78211 336 2

Printed and bound in Great Britain by Clays Ltd, St Ives plc

In loving memory

Phyllis 'Mary' Dyer
27 July 1925–29 June 2011

Arthur 'John' Dyer
30 November 1919–30 November 2011

ANOTHER GREAT DAY AT SEA

I

We were going to be flying to the carrier from the US Navy base in Bahrain on a Grumman C-2A Greyhound: an ungainly propeller plane, more war- or work-horse than greyhound. There was nothing sleek or speedy about it. The sky was doing what it always did at this time: waiting for the sun to show up. The sun is the only thing that happens to the sky in this part of the world—that and the stars which were nowhere to be seen. The temperature was pleasant; a few hours from now it would be infernal. Sixteen passengers, all Navy except for me and the snapper, gathered round the back of the Greyhound—also known as a COD (Carrier Onboard Delivery)—listening to the safety briefing. Our luggage had been weighed and taken away for loading. Despite my protests, I had to hand over my computer bag as well, something I'd never let happen before. It had to be stowed because when we landed on the carrier, when the plane touched down and hooked the arresting wire, we would go from 140 mph to 0 mph in a couple of seconds: the trap, the first of many words that I heard for the first time, or rather the first of many times that I heard a familiar word used in a completely new way. I knew what the trap referred and pertained to—the hook, the arresting wire—but was unsure how to use it. Did we *make* the trap? *Hit* the trap? *Come in for* the trap? The trap: it existed in isolation from other words, abruptly and permanently arrested from the normal momentum of syntax.

Then there was the word 'cranial': in this context not an adjective (as in massage) but a noun referring to the head-, ear- and eye-protectors that were handed out for the flight. Un-noticed, I noticed now, the sky had brightened from grey to blue. We put on our float coats, carried our cranials and filed onto the plane. There were two seats on either side of the aisle—all facing backwards—and two windows on either side of the fuselage, each the size of a dinner plate. It was not the sort of environment in which one could complain about the lack of leg room, though that was one of the striking features of this aircraft. Others were fumes and noise.

The ramp we'd walked up winched itself closed and sealed us in. Further safety checks were made. This involved shining a torch as though to see if there were holes in the fuselage. There must have been more to it than that but holes in a fuselage are good things to check for, obviously. The woman who made these checks was the military equivalent of a flight attendant. She was wearing a sand-coloured flight suit, looked as tough as a woman in an Annie Proulx story. There was nothing of the trolley dolly—nothing 'Chicken or beef?' or 'Doors to manual'—about her, but when she sat down in front of me, prior to take-off, I saw that her hair had been plaited and pinned into a tight bun on the back of her head. The Navy allowed women to keep their hair long. I wasn't surprised, exactly, just pleased that's how things were.

We were not taxiing but a noisy increase in power had taken place and the noise was deafening. I'd thought the noise was deafening when we'd first boarded but back then I didn't know anything about noise or deafeningness. It sounded like the flight of the *Phoenix*. Felt like it too—even though we were not actually moving, let alone flying. This was the moment, evidently, to put on my ear-pinching cranial. Having done that I sat there, strapped tight, struck by the undisguised use of the rivet in the seat in front. Everything in the plane was ripped, scuffed, scratched, stripped. Tubes, pipes, cables and superstructure were all laid bare. Commercial passenger planes from the world's poorest countries outdid this one when it came to frills; even to compare this plane to anything in the fleets of the budget airlines of the West would give a distorting impression of luxury. Passenger comfort was not a factor in any part of the design process.

Having worked itself up to a state of unstoppable intensity the plane accelerated along a runway for so long it seemed that we were attempting the logically impossible: driving overland to the carrier. At last the ground—glimpsed, through the window just behind and to my left—dropped away. We flew over a blur of Gulf but it was neck-achingly awkward, craning backwards to look through the porthole, so I reverted to sitting tight in this silently noisy, vibrating, heavily laden tube, studying rivet patterns.

After forty minutes the bumpy ride became jumpier still as we descended, bucking the bronco air. There was a stomach-draining lurch and heave. We were land— no we weren't! The flight attendant's arm came up in a spiralling lasso gesture to indicate that we had missed the arresting wire and were bolting: going up and around again.

We circled and tilted round, descended again. This time we thumped down and came to a dead stop. Instantly. It was sudden, but not as violent as I'd expected and feared—possibly because we were facing backwards and so were forced into our seats rather than thrown forward and out of them.

The ramp-hatch at the back of the plane was lowered to reveal that we had landed on another world—albeit a world with the same pure blue sky as the one we had left. Rotating radars, an American flag, the island (another old-new word, referring to the bridge and assorted flight-ops rooms rising in a stack from one side of the deck: an island on the island of the carrier). The hatch continued to inch its way down, revealing the flight deck itself, populated by vizor-faced beings in red, green, white, yellow jerseys and float coats. Parked jets—F-18s—and helicopters.

We were here. We had arrived on carrier-world.

I have never known anything like the suddenness of this change. Compare it with the experience of flying from London and landing in Bombay—from freezing winter to eighty-degree heat—at two in the morning in January. Even a change as dramatic as that is gradual: a nine-hour flight; a long and slow descent; taxiing round the airport to the gate; immigration, baggage claim, leaving the terminal. Typically it's an hour and a half before you find yourself out in the Indian night with its smell of wood smoke and the sense of vast numbers of people still asleep. Whereas here, one moment we were travelling at 140 mph and the next we had stopped, the hatch opened and we had entered another world with its own rules, cultures, norms and purposes.

The black-vizored people were either looking our way or scurrying, or lounging or gesturing. Three, in white jerseys and float coats, stepped onto the ramp and told us to follow in single file. They must have been yelling because we stepped out into a silent world—I had not realized until now how effectively the cranials' ear protection worked—in which steam curled and floated along part of the deck. The air was heavy with the smell of jet fuel. Heat blared from the sky and bounced up off the deck. Three more cranial-headed guys in brown jerseys and trousers were swathed in heavy chains like mechanics in the Middle Ages, in charge of a siege engine. We wanted to dawdle but had entered a dawdle-less and urgent world where you do what you are told which was to walk single file to the catwalk at the edge of the deck and then down the steps to the Air Transfer Office (ATO). Already crowded with people preparing to depart, it was soon full to the brim with those who had just arrived.

Ensign Paul Newell, who would be chaperoning us around the boat, squeezed into the room and introduced himself. Always nice to be greeted in an alien world! Especially when the greeter is as friendly, smiling and welcoming as Paul. It was like being met at a resort, conveniently located right under the local airport, with a welcome drink and a garland of flowers to hang around your neck—except there were neither drinks nor garlands. He was wearing a white jersey and sporting something that I would come to recognize as a not uncommon feature of life on the carrier: a form of moustache that has become almost entirely extinct in civilian life. Not an obsolete RAF handlebar extravaganza, just a little under-the-nose, over-the-lip number that had no desire to take itself seriously, that spent most of its time in a state of discreet embarrassment at the mere fact of its continued if meagre existence.

We were ready to go—but we were not ready to go. I had been making notes on the Greyhound and rather than hanging on to my notebook had obediently handed it over to the flight attendant who, as we were about to begin that aborted first descent, chucked it into a kit bag with stuff from other passengers. And it had gone missing. So Paul had to set off on a stationery search and rescue. Why hadn't I just crammed it in my pocket? Because I did as I was told. But by doing as I was told I displayed a lack of initiative which was now delaying—possibly even jeopardizing—the mission.

The other new arrivals were taken to their quarters and those leaving the carrier were escorted onto the flight deck. By the time Paul returned, the snapper and I were the only people left.

'This is all there was,' said Paul. He was holding not a sturdy Moleskine notebook of the type allegedly used and mythologized by Chatwin and Hemingway but a flimsy school exercise book with a green cover and some kiddie's scrawl on the inside pages.

'That's it!' I said, glad to have my vocational identity re-established.

Now we *were* ready to go. Which meant we were ready to begin traipsing through endless walkways, hatches and doorways, some raised up a few inches (knee-knockers), some at floor level. It was like a tunnel of mirrors, and the snapper, naturally, was keen to get a shot of this infinite corridor. That would have to wait. Every ten feet there was one of these open hatches and there was always someone either standing aside for us to go through or walking through as we stood aside—the former, usually. Being a civilian and therefore without rank meant that I was treated as though I outranked everyone. This willingness to step aside, to let me pass, was a demonstration, at the level of courtesy, of a larger point: they were willing to lay down their lives for me, for us. Had the order come to abandon ship I would have been escorted, firmly and courteously, to the first available lifeboat *because I was a civilian*. As well as people stepping aside—one of them with a healing cut across the bridge of his nose and the remains of a black eye—there were always people cleaning. Everywhere you went, down every walkway and stairwell, sailors were washing, wiping, rinsing, dusting, sweeping, scrubbing, brushing, buffing, polishing, shining.

Personally, I spent the rest of my time on the carrier ducking and diving or, more exactly, ducking and stooping. I walked the walkways and stoop-ducked through hatches, always focused on a single ambition: not to smash my head even though there was an opportunity to do so every couple of seconds. It was like staying in a cottage in Wales that had been epically extended and converted to nuclear power. Every time I pulled myself up to full height I was at risk. So I bobbed and weaved, ducked and stooped.

The older one gets the more obvious it becomes that the advantages of being short in this little life greatly outweigh the mythic benefits of being tall. In exchange for a slight edge when serving at tennis and being attractive to tall women (or so we delude ourselves) we spend our time folding our limbs into cars and planes and generally smashing our brains out. My fourteen days on the boat were the stoopingest I have ever spent, fourteen days that rendered the Alexander Technique obsolete, and made nonsense of the idea of good posture. I was on the look-out, right from the start, for other tall men with whom I could bond. Was I the tallest person on the boat? (Did the Navy have a maximum height requirement the way the police or the Army had a minimum one? If so was this ceiling height reduced further in the notoriously cramped conditions of a submarine?)

After five minutes of knee-knock and stoop-walk we arrived at my stateroom. Note the possessive pronoun. Not 'our', 'my'; singular, not plural. *I* was taken to *my* room. The idea of sharing a room had so filled me with dread that, right from the start, I had been lobbying for solitary confinement. That would not be possible, I was told: the snapper and I would share a room with Ensign Newell and three other officers. Six in a room! But we writers need a room of one's own, I claimed, trusting that any grammatical damage would be more than offset—in the eyes of the Navy—by the Virginia Woolf allusion. I like to write at night, I went on, and the sound of my typing would disturb other people. No need to worry about that, came the jaunty response. With jets taking off and landing you become adept at filtering out noise, so a bit of tapping won't disturb anyone. It's not just the typing, I replied (via the mediators who were arranging my stay on the boat). My prostate is shot to hell. I need to pee at least twice a night. What he needs to understand, came the Navy's reply, is that space is extremely limited. Enlisted men and women are in berths of up to two hundred so to be in a room for six is an enormous privilege. What they need to understand, I replied, is that I'm too old to share. I'll go nuts if I have to share. I grew up with no brothers and no sisters. I am constitutionally incapable of sharing. My wife complains about it all the time, I said. Basically, only the Captain and a few other people in positions of high command have their own rooms, came the stern rebuke. Well, maybe I could take the Captain's room and he could move in with Newell and the boys for a fortnight, you know, reconnect with the masses, I emailed back (to my mediator, not intending this to go any further). As the time for my deployment drew near I tried to reconcile myself to the inevitability of sharing a room—I even bought a pair of striped pyjamas—but found it impossible to do so.

Imagine my relief, then, when I was shown to the Vice-Presidential Room in a special little VIP corridor of 'guest suites'. I had got my own room through sheer determination and force of will. I had taken on the might of the US Navy and won. Newell escorted the snapper to their shared quarters, said they'd be back in fifteen minutes, but I didn't give a toss about the snapper: he could have been sleeping out in the open, under the stars on the flight deck, for all I cared. The important thing was that he wasn't sleeping here, with me, even though there was a spare bunk (or rack, as they say in the Navy). That would have been the worst outcome of all: sharing with the snapper, or any *one* for that matter. Sharing a room with one person is worse than sharing with six and sharing with six is in some ways worse than sharing with sixty. But to be here on one's own . . . to have this lovely little room—with a desk, a comfy chair, a basin (for washing in and peeing in at night) and a copy of George Bush Sr.'s daughter's memoir of her dad—was bliss. There was even a thick towelling robe—jeez, it was practically the honeymoon suite, a place where a man could devote himself single-handedly to the maritime art of masturbation.

There was one small problem and it became obvious when I'd been in the room for about three minutes. The crash and thunder of jets taking off. Good God! A roar, a crash and then the massive sound of the catapult rewinding itself or whatever it did. The most irritating noise in my street in London is an occasional leaf-blower. You know how loud—how maddening— that is? The noise here made a leaf-blower sound like leaves in a breeze, the kind of ambient CD played during a crystal-healing or reiki session. This was like a train rumbling over-head. It was nothing like a train rumbling overhead; it was like a jet taking off overhead—or *in* one's head. It was a noise beyond metaphor. Anything other than what it actually was diminished what it was. It was inconceivably noisy but the noise of jets taking off was as nothing compared with the noise of jets *landing*. I thought the ceiling was going to come in. And then there was the shock of the arresting gear doing its business, so that the initial wallop and roar overhead was followed by a massive ratcheting jolt that tore through the whole ship. I knew I was one floor down, directly below the flight deck, and although I wasn't able to work out exactly which noise meant what it seemed that my room was precisely underneath the spot where most planes hit the deck.

How was I ever going to get a night's sleep? Especially since—as Newell explained when he and the snapper came back—this went on all night. I would be here two weeks. I would not get a minute's sleep. Was it the same where they were? No, they were two floors down, Newell said. You could still hear the jets but it wasn't anything like as noisy as here. We were yelling at the top of our voices, not quarrelling, just trying to make ourselves heard.

'And this goes on all night?' I yelled, repeating as a question what I'd just been told.

'Round the clock. It's an aircraft carrier. We're sort of in the business of flying aircraft.'

'Is there still a spare bunk in your room?' I said, not knowing if I was joking. I was torn between relief at having my own room and anxiety about what having my own room entailed.

'You'll get used to it,' said Newell. That's where you're wrong, I wanted to yell back. The essence of my character is an inability to get used to things. This, in fact, is the one thing I *have* grown accustomed to: an inability to get used to things. As soon as I hear that there's something to get used to I know that I won't; I sort of pledge myself to not getting used to it. There wasn't time to yell all this; we had to complete a bunch of forms because, like a man driven mad by people in the apartment upstairs playing thrash metal, I was going right back up to the source of the racket, to the flight deck.

With the paperwork taken care of we stopped off for a safety briefing at the empty ATO—the ATO shack as it was always known—where we were handed cranials and float coats again. The shaven-headed duty officer showed us a plan of the deck, emphasized the importance of sticking close to our escorts, of doing exactly what—and going exactly where—we were told. All pockets were to be buttoned or zippered shut. No loose bits and pieces that could fly away. I could use a notebook and pen but had to make sure that I was holding on to them firmly, not pulling them in and out of my pocket the whole time. And watch out for things you can trip over—there are plenty of them. Any questions?

Loads! But there was no time to ask them. We trooped back up the narrow stairs to the catwalk and were back in the silent world of the flight deck. The empty sea glittered like a brochure ('Ever Dreamed of Holidaying on an Aircraft Carrier?'). The sky was a blue blue, greasy with the reek of fuel (something the tour operators didn't publicize). And there was something dreamlike about it: the cranial silence, for one thing, gave the visual—already heightened by the pristine light—an added sharpness. It wasn't just that the aircraft carrier was another world—the flight deck was a world apart from the rest of the carrier. And everything that happened elsewhere on the carrier had meaning and importance only in terms of what was happening here. Take away the flight deck and the planes and all you've got is a very big boat.

There was a lot to take in—or not to be able to take in. Like the size of the flight deck. How big was it? Impossible to say. It was as big as it was. There was nothing to compare it with. Well, there were people and jets and tons of other equipment, but there was nothing bigger than it—except the sea and sky which always serve to emphasize the lack of everything else. So in tangible, physical terms the carrier was the world and, as such, was all that was the case.

I was not the first writer ever to set foot on an aircraft carrier. One of my predecessors had been hauled up by a sharp-eyed editor for fiddling his expenses. Such things are not unheard of in journalism but this time the editor had him banged to rights: claiming taxi fares during the period when he'd actually been on board the carrier.

'I know,' said the journalist. 'But have you seen the *size* of these things?'

I'd heard another story, about two brothers working in different sections of the same carrier who didn't set eyes on each other during the seven months of their deployment. It didn't matter whether stories like these were factually correct: the truth to which they attest is that carriers are *big*. Big as small towns. Big enough to generate stories about how big they are.

The flight deck is not only big; it is also overwhelmingly horizontal. That's what the carrier has to be: a pure and undisturbed length of horizontality, one that remains that way whatever the sea pitches at it.

The teams in their colour-coded jerseys and float coats reminded me of a time I'd visited the Chicago Stock Exchange with the traders in their colour-coordinated blazers on the dealing floor, all gesturing and clamouring in a repeated daily ritual that made perfect sense, the consequences of which were potentially catastrophic. Here too the functions of each team were clearly differentiated from one another according to a colour code I did not yet understand—except for the brown shirts. We were on one of the most technologically advanced places on earth but the guys in grease-smeared brown jerseys and float coats, draped with heavy brown chains, looked like they were ready to face the burning oil poured on them from the walls of an impregnable castle. The combination of medieval (chains) and sci-fi (cranials and dark vizors) didn't quite cover it, though; there was also an element of the biker gang about them. All things considered, theirs was one of the toughest, roughest looks going. No wonder they stood there lounging with the grace of heavy gun-slingers about to sway into a saloon. Every gesture was determined by having to move in this underwater weight of chain. I couldn't keep my eyes off them. They weren't posing. But in this silent world everyone is looking at everyone else the whole time, all communication is visual, so you're conscious, if you're a guy with a load of chains hanging from your shoulders like an ammo belt, that you're the fulfilment of some kind of fantasy—not a sexual one, more like a fantasy of evolution itself. And they weren't swaggering; there was just the grace that comes from having to minimize effort if a task is to be properly done, especially if a good part of that task involves standing around waiting with all that weight on your shoulders.

The air was an ecological disaster. It was hot anyway, and the heat reared up from the deck, dense with the fumes of jet fuel. Whenever a jet manoeuvred towards the catapults or back to its parking slot or to the elevator there was a wash of super-heated wind, like Death Valley with an oil-gale blowing through it. We were in the middle of the sea and it smelled like a garage with fifty thousand cars in it, each suffering a major fuel leak.

Critics argue that the First Gulf War and the invasion of Iraq were all about America's insatiable need for oil. What did we need this oil for? To sustain our presence here, to keep flying missions. The whole enterprise reeked of oil. Planes were taking off. The fact that cranials insulated us from the ear- and sky-splitting noise emphasized the tremendous forces at work. There was an acute sense of thousands of years of history and refinement—the refinement of the urge to make war and the need for oil in order to do so—converging here.

The purpose of an aircraft carrier is to carry aircraft. Launching and recovering planes is, as Newell had drily pointed out, the name of the game. As a plane prepared to take off, a woman in a green jersey, perched on the edge of a kind of manhole, signalled to other members of the ground crew. Others in green and red signalled to each other with absolute clarity. Everyone was in contact, visually, with everyone else but the jets were the centre of attention, and the pilots flew the jets. All eyes were on the jets. The pilot was the observed of all observers. There was no room for anything even slightly ambiguous. There was a guy near the front of the aircraft, keeping low, making sure he didn't get sucked into the jet intake, and two other guys almost behind the wings—the final checkers—each crouched down on the heel of one foot with the other leg stretched out in front, also keeping low, making sure they weren't hit by the jet blast. How Pina Bausch would have loved to have gotten her hands on this scene! And thank God she didn't! (Same with Claire Denis whose film *Chocolat* ends with a lovely sequence of the gestural language of African baggage handlers and whose *Beau Travail* gazes longingly at the bodies and ballet of soldiers in the French Foreign Legion.) For the beauty of this performance was inseparable from its setting and function. The elaborate, hypnotic choreography on display was devoted entirely to safety, to the safe unleashing of extreme violence. Violence not just in terms of what happened hundreds or thousands of miles away where the planes were headed, but here, where the immense forces required for launch were kept under simmering control.

Up until a certain point a plane can be touched by members of the ground crew. Then the JBD (Jet Blast Deflector) comes up behind the plane. The plane goes to full power—it is only now that one appreciates that the plane, prior to this moment, has been idling, dawdling. The wing flaps are jiggled. Final checks. Thumbs-up between the pilot and the last two members of the ground crew who scurry away, staying low. The plane is flung forward and in seconds is curving away from the end of the carrier, over the sea. In its wake there is a wash of steam from the catapult tracks. After a few moments the catapult shuttle comes back like a singed hare at a greyhound race. A minute later another plane from a neighbouring catapult blasts into the sky.

With the first part of the launch and recovery cycle completed there was an interlude of quietness, though even during the busiest times there had been a lot of hanging about; at least one of the coloured-castes of crew were lounging about in a state of relaxed alertness. John Updike asks, in one of his books about art, if there is such a thing as an American face. I don't know, but looking at the guys on the flight deck, unfaced by cranials and vizors, persuaded me that there is such a thing as an American walk. Even overweight cops have it: an ease and grace, a subdued swagger. It used to be identified mainly with race—a black thing—but now it seems a cultural and national quality.

Through the dazed silence we walked towards the stern of the boat to better observe the planes landing, past the side of the island where a sign warned, quite reasonably:

BEWARE OF

JET BLAST

PROPELLERS

AND ROTORS

All of which were gathered here in great abundance. Over this warning, like the sign of a giant casino, was the white number 77. There was much to see, lots of it on an enormous scale—but my escort was always tapping me on the shoulder, pointing to hoses, pipes, hooks, chains and other small things that could be tripped over.

We could see the planes high up in the blue distance, plane-shaped specks coming round in an immense circle. As they approached the carrier their wings were all the time tilting slightly, first one way and then the other, adjusting, compensating. Three arresting wires—thick as rope but thin and wiry in this context—were stretched across the rear of the deck. On the port side of the boat, very near the back, the landing signal officers—all pilots themselves—communicated detailed refinements of approach to the pilot.

The planes thump down and then, rather than slowing down—as one might reasonably expect—immediately accelerate to full power in case they miss all of the arresting wires and need to go round again, as had happened to us on the Greyhound: a bolter, in the argot. If the hook catches then the arresting wire snakes out in a long V and brings the plane to a halt. The dangers of the operation are numerous and evident. The plane can crash into the back of the ship, slide off to port and into the sea or—worse—slide starboard into the island, people, tow trucks and other parked planes. Every variety of mishap was featured in a book I'd been looking through on the flight to Bahrain: *Clear the Deck! Aircraft Carrier Accidents of World War II*. Unused missiles would shake loose from under wings and be launched into the island. The force of the landing would be so great that a plane already damaged by gunfire would break in two, the back half snagged by the arresting wire while the front part barrelled on down the flight deck. In the worst crashes the plane would become an instant fireball but—and this is what rendered the book engrossing rather than simply horrific—it was often impossible to tell what would happen to the pilot. The plane comes crashing down and, amid the flames, the pilot scrambles out of the cockpit and rolls down a wing to safety. The plane smashes into pieces and the pilot walks away, shaken but otherwise unhurt. But a relatively innocuous-looking crash results in his being killed instantly, still strapped to his seat.

The metaphor that kept coming up in pilots' accounts was that landing on a carrier was like trying to land on a postage stamp (one of the guys I met later on the carrier would use exactly that phrase). Which takes some doing, of course, but if it's daylight, with a steady wind, perfect visibility and the sea flat as a pond it looks fairly routine. But then you throw in some variables: a storm, cross-winds, rain and pitching seas so that looking through the Plexiglas of the cockpit is like being on a trawler in the North Sea. Or maybe one engine's gone. Or both engines are gone. Or you're blinded by gunfire, unable to see anything, taking instructions from a plane on your wing and the LSO, nobody raising their voices, just 'Right rudder, right rudder'—until the last moment when the LSO shouts, 'Attitude, attitude, attitude!'

You can see footage of this stuff, along with a lot more escapes and disasters—recent and vintage—on YouTube. A plane that seems on the brink of stalling, almost vertically, right over the carrier, somehow takes wing again. A malfunction means the navigator has partially ejected and so the pilot has to bring the plane in with his colleague riding on the remains of the cockpit as if at a rodeo. Hearing the LSO yell, 'Eject! Eject! Eject!', pilot and navigator obey instantly, only to see their plane gather speed and fly gamely into the distance like a horse whose jockey has fallen at Becher's Brook.

If all goes as planned, the plane comes to a halt, the tail hook is raised, the arresting wire is released and comes snaking back, helped on its way by crew members who prod it along with brooms to discourage it from even thinking of taking a break. Within seconds it's back in place, kinked and quivering somewhat from the strain of its existence—understandable in the circumstances—but otherwise ready for the next tug of war with an F-18.

2

We trooped back down the stairs, took off our float coats and cranials. In the course of my stay I moved constantly and quickly between the numerous levels below the flight deck, often barely conscious of where I was (didn't have a clue most of the time), but the difference between the flight deck and everything below was absolute. It was like entering the dreamtime up there, a martial realm of the supersonic, where the sky gods G and Negative G had constantly to be assuaged and satisfied. Launch and recovery may have been organized as they were in the interests of efficiency and safety but it was a religious ritual too—a ritual from which it was impossible to return as a non-believer or sceptic even if one didn't understand exactly who was doing what or why (actually that qualifier binds it *more* tightly to traditional religious ceremonies).

Now it was time for another, more ordinary ritual: lunch in the Ward Room reserved for commissioned officers. My anxieties about what life on the boat would be like had not been confined to whether I'd have my own room. I was also worried about the scran, the scoff, the grub. I'm the worst kind of fussy eater. I don't have any allergies and aside from seafood I don't have any generic objections to food types, but I have aversions and revulsions so intense and varied that I struggle to keep track of them myself. I grew up hating all the food my parents cooked, was always being told I didn't eat enough to keep a sparrow alive. That's probably why I'm so skinny, why I joined the lunch queue with some trepidation. Trepidation that turned out to be entirely justified. It was all revolting. The smell of cooked meats and the jet fuel they were cooked in made me heave.

There were salads, yes, but with lettuces represented and disastrously symbolized by the iceberg they were deeply dispiriting. I'm not a principled vegetarian but I was on the look-out for a cooked vegetarian option which I found in the form of spaghetti with tomato sauce. It was almost cold while it was in the serving containers. By the time it had sat on a cold plate for thirty seconds and I had sat down with the snapper, Newell and some friends of his from the Reactor Room, any residue of heat had gone. It was not a pleasant pasta but at least its unpleasantness was all in the moment of consumption; the unpleasantness did not turn into the gag-inducing aftertaste of the big meats. A veteran of assignments in the world's most troubled and least appetizing spots, the snapper tucked in with gusto. He was hungry, the snapper, and he was adaptable. For dessert I had a couple of plums and a yoghurt which, coincidentally, was plum-flavoured though it didn't really taste of anything. It wasn't much of a meal but the sparrow had been kept alive, the wolf from the door. I had got through lunch but I was already—after just one sitting—calculating how many more meals I would have to get through in the course of my stay.

3

After all I'd heard about the size of these carriers I'd assumed there would be an abundance of facilities. Ping-Pong tables—and the prospect of a table-tennis league—were such a cert that I'd actually brought my paddle with me. Badminton seemed likely and, though this might have been a tad optimistic, I even had hopes of a tennis court. The reality is that a carrier is as crowded as a Bombay slum, with an aircraft factory—the hangar bay—in the middle. The hangar bay is the largest internal space on the boat. It's absolutely enormous—and barely big enough for everything going on there.

Just past the hatch through which we entered a dozen men and women in shorts and singlets, all plugged into their iPods, were pedalling away on exercise bikes or running on treadmills. It was like stepping into a future in which the technology of renewable energy had advanced to the point where their efforts powered the whole ship. There was even a statue of someone running: George Bush Sr., of course, in flying suit and kit, scrambling for his plane back in the Second World War when he was a Navy pilot. Fuel tanks were hung from ceiling and walls. Every bit of space was utilized in the same way that my dad, on a smaller scale, maximized space in his garage (never trusting me, as a result, to park his car there after I'd borrowed it). The planes were nuzzled up close to each other. Mechanics were clambering all over them, with special soft moccasins over their boots to prevent damage. Each of the planes had a pilot's name stencilled just below the cockpit where, in the Second World War, Japanese flags or swastikas would indicate kills. But the fact that Dave Hickey had his name here did not mean that it was Hickey's plane for his exclusive use (which made me wonder what the point was of having his name there at all; I mean, when you write your name on the milk carton in the fridge of a shared student house you do it to indicate that it's *your* milk, that it's not for anyone to take a big gulp of or to pour over a bowl of Crunchy Nut Corn Flakes just because they've got the munchies).

I was working my way through this analogy-reminiscence when we were met by Commander Christopher Couch whose businesslike pleasure it was to take us on a tour of this massive—and massively crowded—space. He was in his mid-forties, I guessed, and his hair was cut like everybody else's on the ship. I always like to be in the presence of people who are good at and love their jobs—irrespective of the job—and if ever there was a man in love with his job it was Couch. He began by explaining that the E-2C Hawkeye had an eight-bladed prop and that this had only recently been made possible by advances in materials technology. Made sense. I thought back to First World War biplanes with their twin-bladed props and maximum speeds slightly faster than a bike's. I had no chance to make notes; there was so much to see and it was impossible to keep up with all the model numbers, engine parts, fuels, tools and spools, functions and processes and purposes, many of them dissolving in a torrent of acronyms.

'Wow,' I said during a brief lull in Couch's litany. 'This is the most A-I-E I've ever been in.'

'Excuse me?'

'Acronym Intensive Environment,' I said, feeling both smart and stupid at having risked a first joke in a new place.

'That's a good one,' said Couch in a tone suggesting that there are only bad ones.

Light was pouring in through huge spaces on either side of the hangar: the port and starboard elevators that took planes up to the flight deck. The sea was racing past, a film of light and sky projected from within this vast and silhouetted auditorium. I would like to have watched more of this nautical epic but we were not here to admire the view. Couch's recitation of specs and engine parts, however, was occasionally punctuated by mention of something I could humanly relate to: the beach. It came up several times, this beach, but he wasn't taking a detour into how he liked to spend his vacation—he was talking about 'the long logistical pipeline back to the beach'. Ah, he was still on the job; the beach was the mainland where spares were kept and more complex repairs could be made. I started calculating ways in which I might incorporate this bit of metonymy into dinner-party chat back at London beach. I couldn't think of a single way, but I liked the logic of his usage, the way it performed two tasks simultaneously. It made the deployment seem like a pleasure cruise (if you love your job this much it is sort of a paid vacation) and it also did the opposite: made everything that happened on the mainland seem like buckets-and-spade stuff, a holiday, compared with the serious shit that went on here.

We came to the other end of the hangar, near the very back of the boat, the fantail as they call it in the trade. This was where the jets' engines were tested. At night, a full test would take about eight hours, and it was a source not of amazement but of incomprehension to Couch that anyone would contemplate missing a single minute of this epic performance without concluding that their lives had been thoroughly wasted.

4

The beach came up again, at Carrier Control Approach, which we visited after dark.

'Back at the beach, the field is always there,' said one of the guys, looking up quickly from his screen. It sounded like the beginning of one of those coded radio announcements from the BBC to the French Resistance ahead of D-Day. Either that or a line from a draft of a Wallace Stevens poem. There followed a long interval of silence before whatever was happening on-screen allowed him to resume and complete. 'Yeah, their field is always there. Whereas our airport moves.'

There were sixteen people in the CCA, all zipped up in cosy military jackets, monitoring what looked like a billion dollars' worth of computer screens and radar maps. It was icy as a Vegas hotel and dark as a nightclub. There was even some UV light, emphasizing the white, ghostly, snowy stuff that hung from the ceiling in readiness for Halloween. The temperature had to be kept low because of the equipment but it also meant that there was no chance of anyone dozing off and taking a nap. Just trying to keep warm meant the brain was in a state of constant high alert. The darkness brought out the greens, purples, yellows and reds of the screens. There was an air of relaxed and chilly attention. Someone was drinking coffee from a clear mug with a slice of orange in it—a strange drink. A supervisor stood in the middle of the room, looking over people's shoulders, checking to see how they were doing their jobs. He was a trainee supervisor and someone was watching over him too. Thus the naval hierarchy towers over the boat like the island over the flight deck.

I started to wish I'd worn a thick pullover and wondered what coffee with a slice of orange tasted like. But mainly I was glad I had no one looking over my shoulder, checking on how I was doing my job.

We'd got here half an hour before the birds would start landing. As the time for recovery drew near the atmosphere changed, from attentive to highly focused. With the screens full of data I was reminded, as I had been on the flight deck, of the financial markets, this time with some kind of crisis beginning to make itself felt: a plunge in the FTSE 100, a devastating surge in the NASDAQ. I'd never been in an environment where a slow intensification of concentration was so marked. One of the screens went down. Came back again. I'd heard of the stress of air traffic control, had seen *United 93* in which the controllers manoeuvre aircraft from the path of the hijacked planes. This was more stressful in a way—'our airport moves'—but the number of planes was minimal compared with however many thousands it was that came barrelling in over London every day, hoping to squeeze into a landing spot at Gatwick and Heathrow without circling for hours in a rush-hour holding pattern. The controllers had a distinct way of speaking to the pilots. Firm enough that the idea of not complying did not even occur; relaxed enough that no one would feel they were being bossed around (thereby engendering the reflex urge to do the opposite).

Plasma screens displayed numbers, data and radar info; others transmitted the action on deck as planes came thumping down in the dark, one after another. The picture quality was roughly that of CCTV footage in a Stockwell off-licence. Everything went like clockwork—a phrase which, in this context, sounds several centuries out of date. The birds were all back.

And would stay back till morning. That's right: flight ops finished at about 2140! Newell had known this all along. The talk about planes coming and going like Lionel Richie, all night long, had been just a joke. Everyone was home and would stay home. We were going to have a quiet night in. There would actually be a long interval of what passed, in these parts, for silence.

Lights Out—at ten p.m.—was preceded by an announcement broadcast over the whole ship: a little parable followed by a prayer. It was a nice way of rounding off the day and binding the ship together, those sharing a dorm with two hundred others, officers in a room for six, and the privileged few who had rooms to themselves, who lay in their bunks in the tired knowledge that if they woke in the night needing to pee the basin was only a yard away.

There may have been no jets landing but my stateroom was regularly engulfed by new sources of industrial clamour that earplugs were powerless to keep at bay. I was jolted awake throughout the night but always managed to get back to sleep, partly because the default silence was anything but. It wasn't even *white* noise, more like dark grey shading into black as air, water, heat, coolant and—for all I knew—ammunition or loaves of bread went whistling, howling, surging, clanking, pouring and thumping through the gates and alleys of the carrier's life-support system.

5

Breakfast in the Ward Room was a fried reek of congealed eggs, bacon and other horrors avoided—if not ignored—in favour of cereals, tinned fruit and yoghurt. After that we went right to the source, to the kitchens where it had all been prepared. Showing us round was Warrant Officer Charles Jakes from New York City. He was African American, and had spent twenty-five of his forty-four years in the Navy. In a way that I was becoming accustomed to Charles ran—as opposed to walked or strolled—through a description of his mission and his routines. He was in charge of 112 cooks and 180 food attendants, serving seven places to eat on ship. Increasing quantities of the stuff served in these venues were pre-prepared rather than cooked from scratch (which saved money and time, cut down on staff and accounted, in part, for why meals on the boat were less than appetizing).

The idea, Charles explained, was to go forty-five days without running out of anything. And twenty days without running out of fruit and veg. He took us into a freezer—the size of a Manhattan apartment—and talked us through its contents. Eight thousand pounds of chicken, five thousand pounds of steak, four thousand pounds of hamburger. Waiters in American restaurants always employ the first person singular when announcing and describing the day's specials. 'I have a lamb casserole with a radish reduction,' they will say, as though this interesting-sounding confection has been summoned into existence by his or her descriptive efforts alone. In Charles's case this grammatical habit took on gargantuan proportions.

'I aim to eat my way through everything on the boat,' he said.

'So, going back to the US, I got a million dollars or less left for the last forty-five days.' It made Paul Newman's boast in *Cool Hand Luke*—'I can eat fifty eggs'—seem pitiful, the equivalent of ordering a single softly boiled egg on toast. Speaking of eggs, we moved from freezer to fridge to gaze at 230 boxes of them, which made a total of 575 dozen eggs. This looked like a lot but I calculated that it added up to only just over one egg per person; hence Charles's eagerness to offer reassurance. 'These are not the only eggs. Most the eggs are frozen. These here are just back-up.' Good to know.

En route to one of the store rooms, we passed another chill box which was actually the morgue. 'Ain't nobody in there at the moment,' he said. 'And if there was there'd be a guard outside.' That was good to know too.

As we entered the store room Charles warned that it was in a seriously depleted condition. At the beginning of the deployment stuff would have been piled so high we would not be able to see over the stacks. Now, near the end of deployment which, he hoped, would clean the place out, they were rarely more than four feet high.

First thing we saw was a low-level expanse of popcorn ('they just love popcorn round here'). Beyond the popcorn were six-pound tins (like big pots of paint) of Country Sausage Gravy, Great Northern Beans, Victory Garden Pork and Beans, Popeye Leaf Spinach, Heinz Dill Kosher Sandwich Slices . . .

Like a mother whose son has turned up unexpectedly Charles kept stressing that levels were this low because we only had forty-five days at sea left, that, relatively speaking, there was almost nothing to eat.

Before moving into the bakery we donned little paper Nehru hats. The bakers, from New York, Texas, Chicago and California, were lined up to meet us. They bake eight thousand cakes a week, not counting the ones made for special ceremonies in port (epic cakes iced in the colours of the American flag and the flag of the host country). Our visit was not ceremonial exactly but they had prepared some samples for us. I love cake, cake is my popcorn, and I was glad to be able to tuck in as though it were the snapper, not me, who was always picking at his food like some high-achieving anorexic. It was incredibly hot in here—hot, as Philip Larkin remarked in a different context, as a bakery.

'You're not troubled by the heat in here?' I said.

'Uh-uh,' said one of the bakers. 'Sometimes it gets pretty hot.'

'This is not hot?'

'This a really cool day.'

The visit was as near as I was ever likely to come to being a touring politician or a member of the royal family. I actually found I'd adopted the physical stance of the monarch-in-the-age-of-democracy (standing with my hands behind my back) and the corresponding mental infirmity: nodding my head as though this brief exchange of pleasantries was just about the most demanding form of communication imaginable.

From the bakery we moved into one of the real kitchens: the heart (attack) of the whole feeding operation where Charles resumed his narrative of singular endeavour: 'I aim to prepare maybe four thousand . . . ', 'When I've eaten twenty-five hundred pounds of . . . ' I'd got it into my head that this was not just a figure of speech, and now found it impossible to shake off the image of the genial and willing Charles scarfing his way through piles of meat, potatoes and vegetables, gorging his body beyond its performance envelope, a Sisyphus scrambling up a mountain of food, a calorie-intensive reincarnation of the Ancient Mariner. In its way it was a far more impressive feat of solo perseverance than even the pilots could achieve.

All around were boiling vats as round and deep as kettle drums. A lot of meat was being prepared, plastic bags stuffed full of barbecue chopped pork.

'Hmm, smells good,' I said, instinctively remembering that nine times out of ten the most charming thing to say in any given situation will be the exact opposite of what one really feels. The truth was that the smell was a sustained and nauseated appeal on behalf of the Meat-Is-Murder Coalition or the Transnational Vegan Alliance. But what can you expect when you're in the middle of the ocean with five thousand hungry bellies to stuff, most of them needing plenty of calories to fuel their workouts at the gym?

Our tour concluded with a look at another store room. Notwithstanding Charles's warning about the paucity of supplies, the acute lack of any sense of shortage gave rise to a form of mental indigestion. It was reassuring looking at these tins, seeing them stacked, knowing one would not—*I* would not—be sampling their contents. But what a disappointment if the carrier sank and treasure hunters of the future discovered not the sunken gold and jewels of galleons from the days of the Spanish Armada but thousands of cans of gravy and kosher sandwich slices: the lost city of Atlantis re-imagined as a cut-price hypermarket that had slipped beneath the waves.

6

For the duration of my stay the carrier remained a three-dimensional maze of walkways, stairs and hatches but at some point we always ended up back in the hangar bay—the second most interesting place on the boat (after the flight deck). We passed through there straight after our tour of the kitchen and would do so later the same day, after dark, when it was illuminated by a pale yellow light (less visible from a distance). Now the Arabian sun was peeking through the open expanse of the elevator bay, eager to get a glimpse of whatever was going on in this outpost of industrial America.

Like a buffalo brought down by a lion who then summons the rest of her pride to tuck in, an F-18 was being pecked, prodded and taken apart by a gang of mechanics and engineers. They swarmed over it, drawing metallic entrails from the fuselage, digging into its cockpit and burrowing away in the bowels of the engine. They did this with the utmost care, many of them wearing the soft suede or chamois over-shoes I'd noticed earlier—the heavy industrial equivalent of carpet slippers—to prevent damage to the plane's delicate skin. The concern was reciprocated: little padded pouches were tied to the sharp edges of the plane's fins and wings so that heads were not gashed as people hurried by.

A brown-shirted woman was perched on the wing, cross-legged as if at a festival of future archaeology, concentrating closely on the all-important part she was unscrewing. Having taken the component out of the wing she was now coating it with some kind of grease, glue, anti-freeze, lube or whatever. I apologize for the discrepancy between the precision of the task and the imprecision of my description of that task. I have never liked anything that involves engines, oil or fiddly intricate work even though it is, in a way, in my blood. My dad served his apprenticeship and worked at Gloster Aircraft Company, where one of the first operational jet fighters, the Gloster Meteor, was built. Some days he and his workmates would eat lunch outside, munching their bread-rationed sandwiches, watching planes take off and fly around the shirey skies. (My parents were much on my mind while I was on the boat; my mum had died four months before I came on board; my dad would die, quite suddenly, three weeks after I got back.)

A couple of planes away a fuel cell bladder was being replaced. It looked like a cross between a black python and a massively deflated paddling pool. The work was being overseen by a civilian who, like almost all the civilians on the boat, was ex-military (a Vietnam vet from helicopters, search and rescue). If you met him in the street you would guess straightaway that he had been in the military: a directness, a strength (physical, yes, but also of purpose and identity), an instinct for straight talking that is manifest even when (especially when) silent. A young woman was curled up yoga-ishly on the wing of this plane too, replacing something. The fact that she was wearing a cranial and an oil-smeared brown jersey made her eyes even more luminous. I was glad to have an excuse to talk with her. She wiped her face with the back of her hand, as you do when your fingers are oily. It wasn't exactly a gender-reversal thing going on, but the essential choreography of the scene was being acted out in garages throughout the world: a woman being told what's wrong with her car, in terms barely comprehensible, by a swarthy grease monkey confident of his knowledge and not embarrassed about the oil-smudged pictures of chicks, mainly blonde, who provide a silent chorus of assent when the complexity of the repair and its estimated cost is eventually revealed. No pin-ups like that here, of course: less, I think, because the women on board might find such things offensive than because any man who even considered such forms of decoration would instantly feel like a total dick. A limp dick at that. It's striking how many of the world's little problems—and many of its big ones too—are eliminated by the simplest of solutions: having women around. Just over a fifth of the ship's company were women. Only men in senior positions were old enough to remember what it was like to have men-only boats. One of these explained to me that the main difference, after women came aboard, was 'that the boat smelled a bit nicer because the guys showered more.' Other than that, what surprised him was the speed with which resistance to the idea of gender integration was followed by two related and equally baffling questions: what had all the fuss been about—and why didn't we do this earlier?*

A stranger to the workplace, I needed only a short time on the boat to realize that the workplace—not pubs, parties or clubs—is the great breeding ground of crushes. Over the years I'd developed a strong idea of all the things about office life that I could not tolerate—like using a shared toilet—but it occurred to me now that I couldn't take the drain and strain of having crushes on my co-workers. One was spared that at home alone—but one was missing out on it too.

We chatted some more, me and the bright-eyed mechanic who, it turned out, was from Wyoming. ('Wyoming!' I trilled. 'Really?') It also turned out that another part of our meeting failed to conform to the usual woman-with-car-talking-to-manly-mechanic scenario. Namely that this mechanic had a husband at home who was an ex-Marine. Ah. And they had a four-year-old daughter. Her dad—the dad of the woman I was talking to, grandfather of the four-year-old—was a mechanic

---

*I have recorded what I saw and heard, and my impressions of what I saw and heard. For an investigation of sexual abuse in the US military see Kirby Dick's documentary *The Invisible War*.

and she'd always wanted to be a mechanic herself. It was easy to imagine her as a teenage tomboy, able to mend punctures or tighten a climbing frame that had gone wonky. She was twenty-two now and, looking at her (which I had no desire not to do) I found it difficult to imagine anyone doing what they were doing more contentedly. I dismissed this as soon as I thought it, as soon as I looked around at everyone else, at all the other mechanics and engineers who were going about their business with such concentrated contentment. Even the people who weren't working were working *out,* on the exercise bikes or in one of the fitness classes which seemed a 24/7 feature of the hangar deck. Everywhere you looked, everyone was *doing* something, if not working on the planes then pushing or towing things on trolleys. It was like Whitman's 'Song for Occupations' in an entirely military setting (with a special emphasis on avionics): a vision of a fulfilled and industrious America, each person indispensable to the workings of the larger enterprise, no friction between the person and the task. Which made me think: why not name an aircraft carrier after Whitman? And why stop at Walt? Why not re-brand all the carriers and give them the names of poets? Show me one good reason why the USS *Ronald Reagan* shouldn't be called the USS *Emily Dickinson*.

7

On a boat where everyone worked hard, everyone acknowledged that no one worked harder than the guys operating and maintaining the catapults. The night before we met, Leading Petty Officer Jonathan Dicola had finished work at midnight. Got to sleep at one. Was up at five thirty. Nothing unusual about that—a fairly average day in fact. But it's not just the *length* of the days, the conditions take some beating too. The temperature in one of the rooms connected with the cat—the Launch Valve Room, I think it was called—was 110 degrees (way hotter than the bakery) and some of the guys spent the bulk of their sixteen-hour days in there.

My untrained ear was having trouble keeping up with Dicola's explanation of what the various parts of the cat were called. These, let's say, were failures at the level of the noun. They were exceeded by systematic failures at the level of the verb: what these nouns—these various parts—*did*. But while the workings of the catapult were complex, the consequences of its not functioning properly were easy to grasp. On one occasion, a vertical stabilizer on a jet didn't work, and the plane flipped into the water, killing all five people aboard. On another boat a plane was launched before one of the crew got clear and the wing took his head off. (If it wasn't always clear which of these and other incidents recounted by Dicola had actually been witnessed by him, that is testament to the spirit of shared responsibility that binds together everyone who works in a particular part of the Navy.) Another time the topside PO (Petty Officer) was still underneath when the aircraft went full throttle and sucked him up into the intake.

'Jeez. When did that happen?'

'Maybe '96 or '97. So now they wait for the topside PO to come out and wait for the shooter to say, "Go to military power" and the aircraft goes to full tension. Over the years they learn from those mistakes. We've also had incidents like the chief who wasn't paying attention to what he was doing and ran between the plane and the JBD. The blast blew him up over the JBD. He was tore up pretty good after that. It wasn't funny at the time,' he said, laughing. 'But, you know: *Where was your mind?*'

You can see this incident, or one very like it, on YouTube. Amazingly, you can even see the—or *a*—guy getting sucked cartoonishly into the jet intake. That's quite funny too—because, against all odds, he lives to tell the tale. Instead of getting sucked in, through and out the other end, like meat through a mincer, he caused the engine to blow up and cut out and he came slithering out the way he'd gone in. A few days later he appeared at a press conference, bandaged up like a mummy, but understandably chipper given the implausible fact of his survival.

It made sense to go from the barely comprehensible workings of the catapult to the equally impressive world of the arresting gear. During one of his doomed attempts to explain what was happening, Dicola had likened the cat to a double-barrelled shotgun; at the other end of the boat ABE3 Jefferson Maldonado told me to think in terms of a giant syringe with the cable serving, presumably, as . . . Well, I wasn't sure which part of the analogy the needle fitted into—and not just because of my usual mental shortcomings. I was wearing earplugs, it was difficult to hear, and every few minutes a jet would come screaming and crashing down and it would be impossible to hear *anything*. In spite of all this racket and the attendant jar and crash, the equipment on display—a bunch of massive metal tubes the size of oil pipelines leading into other tubes—did not register the slightest strain or movement. The plane was either a bolter or it had caught one of the other wires (our wire was the third of three).

'I hope we catch one,' Maldonado said, looking and sounding as hopeful and forlorn as he must have done when he and his friends went on fishing trips in the Dominican Republic. He'd moved to New York when he was eleven and joined the Navy when he was eighteen. He was the same age as Dicola and they were both going to put in their full twenty. Which meant—I felt like someone calculating how little time a convicted murderer would serve, outraged by the leniency of the sentence—they would be out in eight years, aged thirty-eight. Looked at in another way, their Navy careers would have spanned roughly the same time as Ryan Giggs's at Man United. The way Jefferson spoke about it, however, comparisons with managers rather than players seemed more appropriate.

'Thing about this job,' he said in one of those epic understatements which seemed such a feature of naval life, 'is that it teaches you to deal with stress.' Immense, almost unimaginable quantities of the stuff.

'If a 747 had a tail hook we could stop that,' he claimed a few moments later. 'That's what they say. I don't know if it's true.' Just in the normal routine of things, planes came in at 140 mph and stopped in 108 feet (or just over a second). There was 2200 feet of cable with a breaking strength of 215,000 pounds. The whole operation was, as he put it, 'maintenance intensive'. The cable had to be replaced every 2500 traps and the bit out on deck that the plane actually hooked on to was good only for a hundred. Given what it was subjected to, I was surprised it lasted that long.

As with the cat, accidents are extremely rare but the effects of a cable snapping are catastrophic. You can see such a thing happening on the USS *George Washington* in 2003. An F-18 comes in to land and hooks the wire which, at the extreme limit of its extension, breaks. The pilot ejects just before the plane skids off the deck and into the water. Then the cable lashes back like a limb-severing whip. A yellow-shirt jumps clear like a kid skipping rope. Incredibly he does this not once but twice as it scythes down anyone and anything else in its path.

Another plane crashed in and this time the equipment slammed, shuttled and recoiled in a din of massively contested force.

'We caught one,' said Jefferson, as if we were sitting quietly on a lake in the Adirondacks—leaves turning brown in the fall, a few clouds—and had hooked a sleek and especially valuable fish.

8

Travellers to Thailand will be familiar with the way that when the national anthem comes on the radio everyone stops whatever it is they're doing—issuing you with a ticket for a train that departs from Chiang Mai for Bangkok in two minutes—and listens. It was the same here with the Captain's daily address to the ship's company. We were in a walkway—of course we were in a walkway, we were always in a walkway—on our way to the chapel, but froze, mid-stride, as the Captain reminded everyone that it was 'a great day to be at sea'. I suppose it was, given the sun, clear skies and the lack of typhoons and incoming torpedoes. What I didn't realize was that the Captain always told everyone what a great day it was. Despite this, he always managed to re-italicize or re-emphasize the 'great', as though yesterday had not been quite *as* great, and today, while in many ways indistinguishable from the interminable days that had gone before, was somehow better and greater, thereby raising the possibility that tomorrow might be *even* greater. It became a standing joke among the crew, and I wondered what would happen when they were making their way back across the Atlantic in November, in Force 9 gales and twenty-foot waves: would he manage to maintain their belief in something they already regarded with a degree of affectionate irony? For now, they expected and looked forward to these daily affirmations of greatness, would have been sorely disillusioned, possibly even mutinous, if he'd summed up the day as merely 'tolerable', 'OK' or 'fine'. There was something very American about this ability to dwell constantly in the realm of the improvable superlative.

The next part of his speech was devoted to publicizing the achievements of the Avenger of the Day, a member of the crew who had been selected for his or her outstanding work irrespective of what that work happened to be.

After this it was down to emailed suggestions from the crew about how things could be improved, how the great days at sea could be made greater. On the one hand, this was a way of turning gripes into suggestions for problem solving: the toilets (the heads) employed a new vacuum system that was prone to blocking and so, at any one time, a number of lavatories seemed to be out of action. This, evidently, was an ongoing source of grievance, one that the Captain was always having to address. On the other hand it was part of the larger ethos of individual and collective improvement that pervaded the ship. I was always seeing little notices exhorting the ship's company to do better. Sometimes these would take the form of generalized encouragement: 'STOP looking at where you have been and START looking at where you can be!' Other times they would encourage the traditional pride of a given department or division—'Setting the standard for excellence'—which bled, naturally, into rivalry. Among the various squadrons of the air wing there were constant and competing reminders and claims to be 'The Tip of the Spear—Stay Sharp'. The Spartan (Helicopter) Squadron's 'Command Philosophy' was broken down into increments:

Take The Fight To The Enemy And Win
Bridge The Gap Between Good And Great
There Is Great Honor In Service To Country
Everyone Is Important
Be Meticulous Stewards Of The Assets We Employ

I loved these and the many other reminders to do better, to improve, but my favourite was somewhat uncertain in intention and effect: 'It's not broke you're just using it wrong.'

Being English, having grown up in a land of out-of-service payphones and faulty trains, my immediate response to this was 'But what if it *is* broken?' What I really liked, though, was the way that the message demonstrated and reflected its own irrefutable truth: that the language, while broke (as opposed to broken), still functioned in spite of being used wrong (incorrectly).

9

When we eventually got to the chapel we were shown around by Commander Cameron Fish—Fish the Bish as he was known during a stint with the Royal Navy. In his late forties, I guessed. He had a narrow face, narrow as the prow of a long boat, but he was at pains to emphasize the breadth of religious belief on the boat. The chapel was there in accordance with constitutional guarantees of religious freedom, not because they were evangelical, he said, sounding more than a little evangelical. Accordingly the chapel changed function—changed religion—depending on who needed it and for what at any given time. The numbers attending were broadly in line with the churchgoing population of the United States—*if* an adjustment was made for the fact that a disproportionate part of the ship's population was from the Christian heartland of the South and the Midwest. There were, the Bish thought, maybe twelve sailors on board who were Jewish by religion, fifteen or twenty Muslims and eight Buddhists, but right now the chapel was being readied for the Pentecostal Bible study class.

The Bish asked Curtis Bell, who was leading the class, if we could stick around. Curtis was wearing a digital camouflage uniform and large spectacles (specially designed, it seemed, for close study of books with many words in very small print). The extreme gentleness of his manner stood in sharp contrast to his heavy, perfectly shined boots. I suspect his impulse, understandably, was to not have us there, but he wrestled quickly with his conscience and, with great courtesy, didn't simply agree to let us stay but *invited* us to do so.

There were only seven people in attendance but that's enough, once the singing starts, to constitute a congregation and choir. One of the women led the singing, setting up the call—'Glory to his name'—joining in the response and moving on to the next call: 'Down at the cross'. I love gospel, especially like this, with no instruments, just uplifted American voices and loose rhythmic hand clapping. To be honest, within thirty seconds the atheist's spirit was moved, tears were trickling down his unbelieving cheeks. Christianity! American Christianity! African American Christianity! The choir of voices, the chain of hands clapping, the promise of freedom and the history of acceptance, resilience and resistance—of breaking the chains—that is there in every line. Oh, I could feel the happiness of it, the joy of being 'wondrously saved from sin' even though the whole idea of sin—and, consequently, being saved from it—was complete nonsense. But it really was a lovely hymn and when it ended I could feel the whole hallelujah-ness of it in myself and the warmth that comes from being in the presence of good people.

Having brought the singing to a close the sister whose name I did not catch moved on to the next phase of the evening.

'I give you all the Glory, all the Honour, all the Praise. Thank you. Thank you for your Holy Spirit. Thank you for sending down your Son to die on the cross.' Thank you for this and thank you for that, thank you for everything, and a special thank you—this was me, extrapolating—for the suffering that gives us the opportunity to thank you for the possibility of bringing our suffering to an end. It was a massively extended and spiritual version of impeccable manners.

'Al*right*! We are in for a treat tonight. Amen. We're gettin' this man full of fire. He's gonna come down and give you what thus sayeth the Lord. He's gonna take you up on each scripture. He's gonna break it down so that you know exactly what this scripture meant. He's not one that takes scriptures out of context. He's gonna make you understand so you're like in kindergarten. Make it plain as day. Amen. He's a true man of God. He follows the spirit, he leads by the spirit. He does everything in decency and orderly. Everything is all of one accord. Amen. I give you none other than brother Curtis Bell.'

Before brother Curtis could take the stand there was another round of singing. It only a took a line—'There is power in the precious blood of the lamb'—and there I was, back in it again, in the small tide of voices ebbing and flowing, calling and calling back.

'*Pow*-er . . .'

'Power *Lord!*'

'*Powe*r . . .'

'Power *Lord!*'

Lovely though it was, the singing had to come to an end so that we could get on with the Bible study part of the evening. Curtis needed a whiteboard and brother Nate was sent to get one. A sister read out a passage of Romans chapter 10, verse 9. 'That if thou shalt confess with thy mouth the Lord Jesus, and shalt believe in thine heart that God hath raised him from the dead, thou shalt be saved.'

To understand this in context, Curtis explained, you had to bear in mind what had come before. For example: 'For they being ignorant of God's righteousness, and going about to establish their own righteousness, have not submitted themselves unto the righteousness of God.'

There followed a confusing exegesis, accompanied by Curtis writing the essentials on the whiteboard: 'Righteousness = justified = redemption = salvation = saved.'

It was a terrible shame. The singing had been so wonderful but now the evening had descended into low-level lit crit of a text that didn't merit any kind of serious scrutiny. It was no better than an aged mullah reducing the complexities of the world to something that could be resolved by a close study of the Qur'an. Curtis was a righteous, spiritual, decent man—he was all the things he had been described as being: a fine man, but he had pledged his light to darkness, had chosen ignorance rather than knowledge and all his knowledge was no more than the elaboration of ignorance. The gap between that and the singing, so heartfelt and full of the spirit, was huge even though the two shared a similar inspiration and belief.

I caught the snapper's eye. We snuck out.

10

I was always self-conscious on the boat, never felt like I was blending in. The crew members were too busy with their long shifts, their chow and everything else that occupied their crowded days to pay me any mind, but I felt as though I stuck out like a hitchhiker's thumb. I kept circling back to Joan Didion's sly declaration of her advantages as a reporter in *Slouching Towards Bethlehem*, one of which was that she was 'so physically small' that people forgot all about her. I, on the other hand, was probably the tallest, thinnest—and, to my chagrin, *oldest*—person on the boat. I was forever in the way, constantly saying 'Sorry' and 'Excuse me' and generally gangling around the place, never more conspicuous than when I was attempting to lurk unseen on the edges of the gym, like Peter Crouch looming into the penalty box.

There was a line to get into the gym and there wasn't a lot of space once you got in. It wasn't just that the room was small—there was also the small matter of every person in it being the size of two people. Arms were as big as legs, necks the size of waists and so on. Three guys were running marathons—on treadmills. The rest were inflating themselves with weights. They favoured baggy shorts and T-shirts or singlets, to prove that however big they got there was always room for further expansion. Even the guys who didn't look that big were plenty big. The bald guys looked like their skulls were pumped. Inked and slinky, the mermaid on a bicep had become six months pregnant by the time a set of reps had been completed.

I've always been intimidated by gyms, have never been able

to enjoy the towel-round-the-shoulder confidence of somebody who knows he can bench-press 250 pounds, or even knows what that means or how much 250 pounds actually weighs. I just know I don't like lifting heavy things, especially since I had this wrist injury which stopped me playing tennis and which means that I've gone from being fit and thin-looking to just a feeble streak of unshouldered manhood whose only saving grace is that he doesn't take up much space, who leaves plenty of room for others—especially now that I was several days into a quasi–hunger strike. I slunk in the corner like a whupped pup, wondering if a visible tatt of a bulldog would have made me look more or less pathetic. The room was bursting with straining flesh and grimacing biceps. Breath came in fierce snorts. There was the clank of heavy metal being laid roughly to rest. I was conscious that I was staring at these Tom-of-Finland arms and chests with an intensity that might have been construed as homoerotic. (There were a couple of women jacked into their iPods, working out, but it was overwhelmingly male in there.) Anthony Benning, the Fit Boss, was standing next to me, wearing a T-shirt and biceps. He had grown up in a military family but was actually a civilian, supervising the exercise programme on ship. From what I could see his job resembled that of a bouncer, stopping people getting in. The gym was filled to capacity so he was operating the one-in-one-out policy that you get at overcrowded nightclubs. I didn't know what to say but, feeling I ought to ask a question, said:

'How big can a human arm become before it stops being a limb and morphs into something else?'

'Excuse me?' he said, and so I changed my tune and came up with a different question, still physical, but less meta.

'I said, "Are you the fittest person on the boat?"' I said.

'Lot of people fitter than me.'

'Lot of people fatter than me,' I quipped back. Then, fearing the conversation was taking on a slightly unhinged quality, I asked him about the food, its compatibility or otherwise with fitness and well-being.

'Most people eat healthier on the ship than they do at home,' he said. This seemed stodgily plausible. I nodded in a way I hoped would not seem tofu-snooty. We stood without speaking, arms folded—his massively, mine meagrely—like spectators at a muscular orgy.

'Don't suppose you know anyone I can score some steroids from, do you?' I said after a while. He smiled, shook his head, said he'd ask around.

'Well, better make room for somebody else,' I said, squeezing past him as though I'd just shattered the world bench press and reps record.

11

Everybody on the boat worked long hours, everyone did so uncomplainingly and without obvious signs of stress—though some looked plenty tired—but no one would have greeted news of the introduction of a new thirty-hour-day with quite the cheer of Commander Kimberly Toone, the ship's senior medical officer. She was that rare thing: a high-energy person with nothing even slightly manic about her; she just happened to be in a very good mood all the time—probably from the day she came bouncing into this world. On her desk she had a jar filled with sweets; I kept helping myself to them in the course of our talk, chewing constantly, conscious that this was the nicest taste I'd had in my mouth since I came aboard.

'So,' I said, munching away sweetly. 'Tell me all about it—the mishaps, the accidents, the injuries. What's an average day like here in the Crimea?'

'I'd say on average there are four accidents a day. Ten minor accidents on the busiest day. Mainly it's things like crushed fingers, tractors running over toes. On this deployment there's been nothing life threatening in terms of accidents.'

The crushed fingers thing came as no surprise. Just as homosexuals have a highly effective gaydar so, over the years, I've developed a kind of sixth sense in the realm of health and safety. I detect potential accident and trouble spots without even having to try. I knew that the hatches, particularly the ones requiring a quite complicated manoeuvre with levered handles, were lethal when it came to fingers (especially if there was a difference in air pressure on the other side). That was why, whenever possible, I let Ensign Newell or the snapper open and close them as we made our rounds. They would never have guessed what I was up to; it just happened that my hands were always full (with notebook, water bottle and pen).

'And then there are the facial injuries,' Kimberly went on breezily. 'People who aren't paying attention and walk into ailerons or horizontal stabilizers and whack themselves in the nose. Some of those are like a knife edge. We had a guy recently who cut himself right across the nose.'

'I've seen that guy,' I said. 'On my first morning!'

'That might have been the guy who was hit in the face with a beer bottle when we were in Jebel Ali, so that's a different story.'

'Ah.'

'In terms of accidents what happens here is pretty much what you'd expect from an industrial environment.'

This was not the first time that I'd heard the carrier described as 'an industrial environment'. In my teens the phrase 'military-industrial complex' used to come up quite a bit, and I suppose, strictly speaking, we were in a military-industrial environment, but the thing that struck me now was that I had never wanted to spend even a minute in an industrial environment (they are noisy, greasy, dangerous places) and yet I had signed up for this, a place that was also unusually vulnerable to infections and outbreaks (which, in my normal life, I am at pains to avoid). In terms of the risk of infection, being on a carrier is like living permanently on the tube—albeit a tube that hardly ever stops at a station and takes on very few new passengers, so maybe this analogy was not so helpful after all. Still, Kimberly continued, getting people inoculated against flu as soon as the vaccine became available was a matter of some urgency.

'You know, we got everybody vaccinated with a flu shot in seventy-two hours. Five thousand people in seventy-two hours, that's a lot of shots.'

'The needle must've been pretty blunt by the end of that.'

'Bent like a coat hanger. And gummed up with blood pretty good too. But our big success this deployment was the Bahrain bug.'

'Tell me about the Bahrain bug,' I said, reaching into the jar for more sweets. Instead of taking them singly, I was now just scooping them up by the handful.

'We had a diarrhoea outbreak when we left Bahrain back in August. Epidemic viral gastroenteritis.' Kimberly had been smiling throughout our conversation, but now her face lit up as though she were about to tell me that her daughter had won a full scholarship to Harvard. 'Fifteen to twenty per cent of the crew were affected—or at least came to medical. Plus there were lots of emergencies stemming from the bug: people getting dehydrated and passing out because it's a dehydrating environment anyway. I have a master's degree in public health so this is the kind of thing I know about—and what I know is how simple it is to deal with. The big thing that helped us fight the bug was turning the spoons around so the crew weren't allowed to serve themselves in the mess halls. That stops it spreading. If one person who has the bug touches the spoon he passes it on to everyone behind. We had a bit of a fight with the sailors. They're told what to wear, when to sleep, what to do. Eating is one of those things that, it's like, "It's me, it's my time". And you're taking away their ability to choose, taking away that last little bit of independence. So we got a lot of pushback. But within three to four days our symptoms were cut in half.'

I was acutely conscious of two things: first, that I'd been clawing away at the candy jar with my bare hands; second, relief that I'd not been on board for the Bahrain bug, especially given the problems with the vacuum system that kept putting the toilets out of action. I was already investing a lot of energy into not banging my head and a good amount of cunning into making sure that if anyone's fingers got crushed by hatches they would be the snapper's or Newell's, rather than mine. After this meeting with the MO I added another string to my bow of precautions: always looking out for anti-bacterial dispensers, never passing up a chance to sanitize my hands as if we were docked at the harbour in Camus's Oran, a city in the grips of plague and pestilence.

12

The bridge: that much-filmed spot where John Mills would stand, soul and head bared to the elements in the Battle of the Atlantic, wearing a soaking wet polo neck, worn down by the war, 'this bloody war' as he called it. How deeply that war—the Second World one—seeped into our pores and brains when we were kids. I remember my friend Nigel Raeburn and I coming home from school on the bus: top deck, front row—the bridge! We were twelve at the time and Nigel started singing, 'When this bloody war is over . . .' He wasn't just singing a song the way he might have sung the latest hit single by Rod Stewart; he was channelling the battered spirit of British wartime resilience. It was as if a time machine had taken him back to 1941 and he was lost in a reverie about the loneliness and futility of being separated from his full-bosomed sweetheart who might have been Vera Lynn herself. Perhaps the strangest part of this story is not that he was able to slip back thirty years in this way but that I am able to skip back forty so easily. I can hear and see him now with his ginger hair and pudgy lips, as clearly as if I were there, on the bridge of that bus rather than on the bridge of the USS *George H.W. Bush*.

The *Bush* bridge was sealed in, of course, not like the open-air one on which John Mills gallantly performed. A dozen people were up there, all doing something. A lot of that doing was looking out of the window and some of the looking was being done with binoculars. Planes were taking off relatively silently beyond the glass, specimens released from a technological aviary. It was all contemporary-looking but steeped in tradition too—as when a sailor suddenly piped up, 'Captain's on the bridge!' Like everyone else I stood to attention, approximately. Captain Brian Luther was here to make his daily address to the ship's company but first he admonished someone on the bridge for a gross impertinence: 'I don't wanna hear anything about the Pittsburgh Stealers on my bridge.'

The Captain began his address by confirming what everyone knew: that it was 'another beautiful day at sea'. The trick was not simply to repeat exactly the same thing but to re-establish the same idea—another great day at sea—through slight variations. Like this the ship's company hung on his every word, always curious to learn exactly which version of excellence had been achieved and experienced on a particular day, thereby imbuing it with a specialness within the unbroken continuum of always-improvable-on greatness.

The Avenger of the Day—this beautiful day—was Stremmle, a lanky twenty-two-year-old who the Captain invited to sit in the big chair 'and drive the boat for a bit'. While Stremmle was driving the boat the Captain explained to the ship's company that he (Stremmel) had volunteered for extra shifts, had done this and that, and was—this too was part of the daily incantation—'an outstanding example of freedom at work'. Another nice part of this little ritual was that the Avengers got to call home to tell their sweethearts or parents that they were here and being honoured in this way. The Captain's Avenger of the Day announcement ended not with a hierarchical nod of approval but a nicely democratic 'Well done, shipmate'. In that instant Captain and Avenger were equals—and the promise was held out that any of the five thousand people on board had the opportunity to attain a similar relationship and, ultimately, to become not simply the beneficiary of the award but its bestower.

13

At dinner that night I fulfilled one of my investigative ambitions: I met someone taller than me. Taller and wider. HMSC Mitchell was a vast African American who seemed to have been definitively reconfigured by living on a carrier. You hear it said of certain stocky, well-built men that they don't have necks. Well, Mitchell *had* a neck in the sense that he used to have one but since it was as useful, in the stooping corridors of the carrier, as a giraffe's he had managed, courtesy of an accelerated, one-person form of evolution, almost entirely to internalize it, to bury his neck within his shoulders. This must have caused some discomfort but that, presumably, was less than the pain of repeatedly smashing his head open (though that, to judge by an abundance of scars and bumps, had not been entirely avoided). Was the procedure reversible? When he got off the carrier and was back in the open skies of Norfolk, Virginia, would his neck re-emerge as if from hibernation and allow him once again to walk as tall as nature had intended?

He was so big, another member of the crew claimed, that he'd had his rack specially extended which seemed extremely considerate of the Navy. Mitchell laughingly denied this. Nope, he had to suck it up. Just folded himself into his rack like he was a fold-up bed and learned to sleep without too much wriggling around.

The removal of the possibility of complaint—of being forced to suck it up—can have a liberating effect. There was no Wi-Fi on the boat and the usual email accounts—Gmail and Hotmail—

could not be used. So I had to go through an elaborate procedure to obtain a special naval email address which I would check after dinner each day in the ship's library. The library was somewhat of a sanctuary, though you might not have guessed it from the TV which was always showing films at high volume. No, the clue lay in the detailed additions to the 'Rules to Live By'. These Rules declared that

> *Any display of affection between shipmates while on*
> *board the ship . . . is strictly prohibited.*
> *Out of the way places on the ship are off limits for any*
> *male-female meetings.*

Here, in the library, the forbidden specifics were spelled out:

> *Close proximity viewing of movies on computer or DVD player*
> *(Must maintain 1 foot distance between individuals.)*
> *Close proximity "hanging out"*
> *Leaning against or on another person*

It was well-stocked with books, the library, but the main attraction was the availability of laptops even though they were only rarely available. There was always a wait for one to become free and then a further wait to get online successfully. My account was particularly hard to use and, on this occasion, it froze almost as soon as I had logged in. I phoned the IT guy who said it would be necessary to reset my account which would take about fifteen minutes—by which time I had to be elsewhere for a meeting. This is the kind of thing which, in normal life, can make me go completely crazy. That is an understatement. A fraction of this annoyance can lead me to do something seriously . . . 'childish' is the word favoured by my wife. Childishness, here, was not an option. Inside I was screaming but I didn't howl or whine, didn't even raise my voice. I was haemorrhaging tears, my head was a balloon pumped full of blood. People talk about the red mist but I could sort of see the red blood welling up behind my eyes like the surface of the ocean viewed through a sub's periscope. But I sucked it up. I pushed my chair back and stood up from the computer. I imagined myself picking up the chair and swinging the chair into the computer; instead I stepped up to the counter and spoke to the librarian politely. I said please and thank you. I had the face of a serial killer. I sucked it up.

Good job I did, because the person I had to meet was none other than Brian Luther—the Captain. He and two friends were sitting in fold-up chairs on a starboard-side catwalk, smoking cigars in the dark. The sea was nothing but darkness. I could not see anyone's face, just the red orbs of their cigars. Then a crew member rigged up a line of blue fairy lights; it was still hard to see but in a soft romantic way. With the Captain were Jeff Davis—Air Wing Commander: the Captain's equivalent, in charge of the planes and the flyers in the same way the Captain was in charge of the boat and the sailors—and Jeff's deputy, Dan Dwyer. Jeff was fifty, Dan forty-four and the Captain forty-nine. I had succeeded in meeting someone taller than me but, even among the most senior officers on the ship, had not yet found anyone older. We sat all in a line, facing out to sea.

The Captain, I discovered in this intimate setting, was someone whose life embodied compromise and scaled-down hopes. He'd wanted to be an astronaut but had settled for bossing an aircraft carrier (or 'driving the ship' as he always put it). One of the things that had distracted him from his astronaut ambition was falling in love with 'the ballet' of carrier aviation. It was reassuring to have my first impressions of the flight deck confirmed by a higher authority. Like his two buddies the Captain had notched up a thousand hours as a carrier aviator; Jeff and Dan had 'flown fighters across the beach in combat'. They were still flying missions every other day but they were getting towards the end of their flying days. I asked about this, about the relationship between growing old—or becoming middle-aged—and advances in technology which were transforming what it meant to fly a plane and be a pilot. That was true, the Captain said, but their experience counted for so much. Dan, he pointed out, had over a thousand arrested landings to his credit. That added up to a lot of skill, a lot of thrills—and a whole load of scares. I could see the shapes of their faces, slightly illuminated when they puffed on cigars, but could not tell who was speaking. It didn't matter because they all agreed on one thing: everything about the job was fun. They were like kids, the three of them, still delighted that they got to drive and fly around in these incredible machines. But they were in earnest, also, about dedicating themselves to a life of service, to something (though I don't know which one of them said this) 'greater than self'.

'It's a respectable profession,' said a voice in the blue-tinged darkness.

'An honourable profession,' said another.

I had not been on the boat long but I understood what they meant and believed in it absolutely. I asked what they were doing and where they were when the 9/11 attacks happened.

'I was on the *Enterprise*,' the Captain said. 'We'd left the Gulf on 9/9 and were headed south to port call in Africa. Then 9/11 occurred and the CO of the ship watched what was going on. He turned the ship around and started steaming towards the coast of Pakistan. As they felt the ship turning the whole crew cheered. When things happen the president says, "Where are the carriers?" We are part of world events, part of history as it's made. If something happens we go to where history is made. We're the tip of the spear.'

'But you don't need to talk to old guys like us about this,' Jeff said. 'There are a lot of people on this boat who've been in ten years now. Kids who were in the heartland, who had never seen the ocean, who, when 9/11 happened said, "I'm gonna make a difference." No need for a draft or recruitment.'

'About those kids,' I said in the direction of the Captain. 'Was the Avenger of the Day your idea?'

'No, that was up and running before I took command. But it's interesting because normally these kids wanna stay *away* from the Captain!' How I *liked* these guys, the ease with which they went from talking absolutely seriously about serving their country to just joking around. 'What I introduced was the phone call home. But that can backfire too. The mom picks up and she's like, "What did he do now?"'

We sat there in a row, chuckling, looking out at the night-dark sea.

14

I had perfected my end-of-day routine. At 2140 I put on my thick towelling robe and flip-flops, trotted to the head and showers where I showered quickly, dried off and darted skinnily back to my room. For ten minutes I lay on my rack reading Norman Polmar's *Aircraft Carriers: A History of Carrier Aviation and Its Influence on World Events*, volume I (1909–1945), until the little story and prayer came over the Main Circuit just before Lights Out. Sometimes the stories were jokey (a bit from *Charlie Brown* about a field of pumpkins and nothing but sincerity as far as the eye can see); other times they were a bit cheesy: stuff about dancing like no one was watching, loving like you'd never been hurt. But I always liked the next bit: the prayer, when God would be thanked for granting endurance to those on watch, for bringing rest to tired eyes and those suffering from exhaustion. After that I turned off my bunk light and basked in the luxurious fact of being in my own room with its guarantee of sleep and rest. Some nights I lay awake for ages, thinking how nice it was, having my own room in which I could enjoy a night's sleep.

And some nights I lay in my bunk thinking about the weird perk of having ended up here. Asked, nine months earlier, if there was 'somewhere unusual and interesting' I'd like to be writer-in-residence I didn't hesitate: Sir, an American aircraft carrier, sir!

It had to be American: circumstantially, because these days we—the British—don't even have a carrier; personally, because of the accents, the audible symptoms of the top-to-bottom, toff-to-prole hierarchy that is so clearly manifest in the British military. If I've been in America for a while and am about to fly back to LHR from JFK or LAX my heart sinks when I hear again a substantial concentration of British accents. To have locked myself away on a British aircraft carrier—if one had existed—would have been to have condemned myself to being on a shrunken version of our island kingdom (which is often thought of as a kind of gigantically expanded carrier). Sitting in on a US ship, on the other hand, would be like staying in a small town in America (albeit one organized along unusually clear hierarchical lines), surrounded by American voices, American friendliness, American politeness, American *Americans*. That, I knew, would be a source of pleasure and happiness.

The attraction of a carrier—as opposed to a US battleship, or bank or hospital or whatever other institution might have hosted me—was similarly straightforward. I was born in 1958 and, as that earlier story about me and Nigel Raeburn on the bridge of the bus illustrated, my childhood was dominated by the Second World War. I loved planes, military planes especially, the Battle of Britain particularly. Like almost every other boy of my age, long hours spent making and blotchily painting Airfix models meant that I had an encyclopaedic knowledge of Second World War aircraft. This plane-spotter's know-how was backed up by a limited if sometimes deluded idea of what these planes were used for: Stukas dive-bombed Polish cities, Hurricanes and Spitfires fought off Heinkels and Dorniers in the Anglo-blue skies of 1940, the de Havilland Mosquitoes of 633 Squadron attacked a factory making fuel for V-2 rockets, Lancasters busted the Mona dam and destroyed industrial targets deep in the Ruhr valley, bomb-laden Mitsubishi Zeroes plunged into US aircraft carriers. Within the narrative of the Second World War—to liberate the world from the tyranny of Hitler and the Japanese—I also had a sense of the larger strategy in which these aircraft played a part. This expanded understanding pretty much ended with the coming of the jet fighter (Messerschmitt 262 and Gloster Meteor) and the end of the war. I kept making models of later jets—the Dassault Mirage, the Blackburn Buccaneer, the English Electric Lightning among others—but I didn't know what they did or where or why they were deployed. They just flew incredibly fast and looked amazing on Perspex stands.

My favourite model was the two-seater McDonnell F-4B Phantom, a jet that was both sleek and densely laden with armaments. And not just armaments: it was also dense with decals: NAVY on the side of the fuselage, red lightning bolt jagging along the top and up the tail fin, star-and-stripe roundel on the wings and near the jet intake. The box showed a Phantom about to take off from a carrier, after-burners ablaze, while steam rolled across the flight deck from a launch that had occurred a few seconds earlier—exactly the kind of scene that I would end up witnessing, daily, on the *George Bush*. As with other jets—the Blackburn Buccaneer or Dassault Mirage—I had no idea what real Phantoms were doing in the skies over Vietnam at the very moment that I was making 1:72 scale versions of them at home. Obviously some kind of understanding—destroying a country, winning battles in a losing war—came later but the aesthetic intoxication of military jets never went away. Even while my friends and I were busy opposing the Falklands War we also felt a flush of late-imperial, aeronautical pride that the Sea Harriers ('I counted them all out and I counted them all back') launched from HMS *Invincible* and HMS *Hermes* performed so effectively against the Argentinean defences. In the early 1990s, after the collapse of the Soviet Union had rendered a lot of military planes operationally redundant, I jumped at the chance—a kind of inverse ejection—to fly in a MiG-29 over Moscow.* That, as the kids say, was pretty cool, but since all of the devastating power and glamour of military aviation was concentrated on a

---

*In the unlikely event of anyone wanting to know more about this or my earlier love of model aircraft, see the essays 'The Wrong Stuff' and 'The Airfix Generation' in either *Otherwise Known as the Human Condition* (US) or *Anglo-English Attitudes* (UK).

carrier, I wanted to be there too, at the tip of the spear—or to have a ringside view of it anyway.

And maybe something else was at work too. As a boy I had loved war and soldiering. I grew out of this entirely healthy infatuation and, when I was a student, my life began to assume the opposite of a military bent in that, through a combination of passive ambition and luck, I became, as adults say, my own boss. Freed from the chain-of-office-command, I acquired a weird kind of self-discipline—all but indistinguishable from self-indulgence—that became second nature. But during afternoons when I could not bring myself to write and in the evenings when I did not feel under any compulsion to try, I read more and more about the military, becoming increasingly fascinated by a world that was the polar opposite of my own. I got particularly obsessed with reading about the US Marine Corps to the extent that, in a softly lit, armchairish sort of way, I began to wonder if, in another life, I might have joined the Marines, might have been a jarhead and had 'Semper Fi' tattooed on a properly muscular forearm. In fact, when I said I didn't hesitate about wanting to be on a carrier I was not being quite accurate; I hesitated between the possibility of being writer-in-residence on a carrier or in Camp Pendleton, the Marine base near San Diego, California. I hesitated and dithered. I didn't know if they'd even let me into Pendleton (where the food, I'm guessing, is even worse than on the *Bush*) but in the end I opted for a carrier. It panned out, they allowed me aboard, and that's where I ended up, in my bunk, in my own room, drafting this passage.

15

What a difference a consonant and vowel can make. Having been up on the bridge the previous afternoon, the following morning I was taken down to the brig. I'd heard the word before, in films, never in real life, and now I was seeing one, seeing a brig (though the word seemed to demand that it was preceded by a solid and definite article, not an indefinite article, as if there were only one brig—*the* brig—that somehow manifested itself in different ways, in different settings). The brig: the word had its own glamour, was a high-security metaphor for the kind of charismatic rebellion embodied by Jack Nicholson in *The Last Detail*, or—extending the linguistic catchment area slightly—Paul Newman in the box in *Cool Hand Luke* or Steve McQueen languishing in the cooler in *The Great Escape*. Physical confinement, in such cases, exists in order to demonstrate a refusal to be psychologically confined, the uncrushable freedom of the unruly spirit that will not submit to authority.

In charge of the brig was Petty Officer Young, a small no-nonsense woman with metal-framed glasses and hair pulled back in a tight carceral bun. She'd been a mom at twenty, did two years of college, married at twenty-eight, was a teacher's assistant, had been in landscaping and retail and joined the Navy at thirty-two. It was like a life lived backwards, somehow, even if she was only now achieving her long-time ambition: 'I always wanted to be in law enforcement.' A strange ambition until you consider that quite a few people pursue the opposite goal—of law-breaking—from a young age with similar dedication.

Before I looked at the cells Petty Officer Young explained to me what you needed to do to end up here. Minor offences meant you were put on restriction.

'What sort of offences are those?' I asked.

'Falsifying your log books, persistent lateness, sleeping on watch, talking back to an officer, disrespecting an officer, calling him a bad word, telling him he's acting like a bad word.'

'And what about that word "restriction"? What does that mean?'

'Restriction requires that you muster and roll call several times a day. You've probably seen them lined up in the hangar deck.'

I had indeed, just a few hours earlier, while an exercise class was in progress and everyone else was going about their business of fixing up planes. They were standing at attention, clearly regretting the added increment of inconvenience to which they were being subjected. Everything about the Navy system of discipline advertised the advantages of not getting deeper into trouble. Better to suck up being on restriction and then get off restriction and enjoy that as a pleasure and a bonus rather than sucking up whatever comes your way at the tier below restriction. Better to improve than to get worse. But not everyone does.

'Miss three musters and you're here on bread and water for three days. More serious offences, you'd skip restriction and come straight here.'

'Such as?' I asked (picturing myself being frog-marched to the brig for throwing a chair through a computer screen).

'Assaults. Homicidal tendencies. If somebody on the flight deck got really mad and tried to shank someone with a screwdriver they'd be here.'

'Has that happened?'

'It has not. But it could.'

Hungry for gossip, for anecdotes, I asked Petty Officer Young if she could give me examples of serious stuff that had happened.

'With all due respect I have no authority to describe or discuss particular cases.'

I felt like I'd been told off, like I'd taken a tentative step towards trouble, towards the brig (in which I was already standing). I've always hated getting told off. *If you're not going to tell me then what the bad word am I doing here?* I thought to myself. Petty Officer Young, meanwhile, was telling me about another category of inmate: enemy prisoners of war. I'd like to have seen some of *them,* maybe even poked at them with a stick from behind the safety of the cell bars, but the brig, today, was devoid of all prisoners, friendly or hostile (pronounced American-style, as in 'youth hostel').

Within the brig there were two individual cells and a large dorm cell that could sleep fifteen. I studied both with the appraising eye of a real estate agent. While somewhat basic the accommodation benefitted from high levels of security. There were no windows, but since almost no one on board had an ocean view this did not represent a diminution of privileges enjoyed elsewhere on the boat. In a sense the brig represented not a removal from but an extreme concentration of the experience of being on the carrier. For everyone except the pilots and helicopter crews the carrier was a kind of prison ship. So I guess the real punishment of being in the brig would be the annihilating boredom. There was a TV in the dorm cell. I am not a lawyer, but it's possible that access to TV is a constitutional right, even if having it on seems a human rights abuse, conceivably a form of torture.

We were joined by Petty Officer Heath. He'd signed up for the Navy at twenty-three because 'the environment I was in at home didn't have much promise.' Prior to the Navy he'd built trailers, driven semitrucks, just bouncing from one thing to another. He was twenty-eight now, with four kids back home.

The ironic life of prison guards was plain to see. They had no guests but were obliged to spend their days in the joint. They were running a deeply unsuccessful establishment whose lack of business was the price paid for the great successes achieved elsewhere in town. From my point of view it would have been much better if the jail had been occupied, by sailors in the process of being punished or, ideally, an Al-Qaida suspect, one of those guys with a gleaming black beard and a gentle expression whose eyes burned darkly with some implacable faith and who—for all we knew—was just a devout Muslim and a caring father.

'So what do you do when you've got no customers?'

'Before you got here I was touching up the paint,' said Petty Officer Young.

'I clean,' said Petty Officer Heath.

The place was plenty clean, and resolutely empty, one of the few places on the ship whose intended purpose rendered it (compared to the kitchens working flat out, the flight deck taking its daily pounding) redundant. It was a small space, so small that it felt strangely full of itself, crowded with unutilized function. The brig even contained its own caption in the form of an unused sponge, on the spotless sink, with CELL BLOCK printed in large letters. The last thing I did before getting out of the brig— thereby risking another telling off—was to ask if I could have that sponge, take it home as a souvenir.

16

After doing time in the brig—about forty minutes—I wanted to meet someone who'd been in trouble or, at the very least, had been on restriction. With his usual unfailing efficiency Ensign Newell promptly took me to meet YN2 Sonia Martin.* When I came into her office Sonia wouldn't shake my hand. Ah, attitude, right from the start! Because she had a heavy cold. The opposite of attitude, then, more like a highly developed sense of citizenship and disease-prevention of the kind that stopped the Bahrain bug taking over the whole ship, turning the p to t. In London I've often gone to literary parties and been greeted with a kiss only for the kisser to then declare, 'I've got a terrible cold.' I was therefore well disposed towards Sonia right from the start— though, naturally, I kept my chair as far away from her as possible. So, what had she done to get put on restriction?

'I disobeyed a lawful order.'

I extended my right arm, hand outstretched as if to say, 'We are all friends here, please speak freely, it's all off the record'; with my other hand, I took notes.

'I was found in a space with my then husband. We were sleeping but . . . He was getting out of the Navy, he was on restriction so he was stuck on the ship and I stayed with him.'

There was quite a bit to unpack in this capsule summary. I asked Sonia to back up, to give more details. They had met on the ship, he was getting kicked out and they got married shortly before this was due to happen. The ship was in port at San Diego . . .

* Not her real name.

'Why was he getting kicked out?'

'Doing drugs. He popped some meth together with . . .'

'Other drugs?'

'Other friends. The policy was zero tolerance then, like now. But people did it before and they kept doing it and I fell in with that crowd. Afterwards he wanted to continue doing drugs and I wanted to continue doing the Navy so our two paths did not go together.'

'What was his job in the Navy?'

'He was a damage-control man.'

'That doesn't seem the most appropriate line of work for someone with his recreational interests.'

'I know. Why he ever joined the Navy I'm not quite sure.'

Everyone on the carrier smiled while they talked to me; some laughed, but Sonia's answers were punctuated with giggles as though she was constantly reminded of the underlying absurdity of things. That might be one of the enduring pluses of dabbling in drugs. But how about being on restriction—what was that like?

'It sucked and the stigma of everyone seeing that you were on restriction was embarrassing. The extra work wasn't so bad. I wasn't able to go home for Christmas. I didn't get to go home for the holidays and that sucked.'

Before now I had not made a connection between things sucking and sucking things up. Now it seemed obvious that something sucking was a precondition to its being sucked up. Though of course the number of things one had to suck up was not limited to things which sucked. And the things that sucked most— like getting sucked up into the air intake of a jet engine—were things that could not be sucked up. I had drifted off somewhat so I was glad that our conversation was interrupted by someone who came in with a couple of work questions for Sonia. I looked around the room but there was nothing to notice in these ship-board offices. But hang on . . . Wasn't that a mirror and a rolled-up dollar bill on the far side of her desk . . . ? Ha ha, no, of course not, it was just a note I made to myself, for comic effect, while Sonia was talking to her colleague.

When her shipmate's queries had been dealt with Sonia resumed her story and I gave her my full attention again. It was only after being on restriction—near the end of her third year—that she'd decided to make a career of the Navy. Before that she'd intended getting out after the four years she'd signed up for—though she still credits that initial decision to join with turning her life around.

'I would either have been dead or in jail if I hadn't joined the Navy. I was living with a dealer at one point.'

Again, clarification was needed. 'Living with him romantically?'

'He wasn't a boyfriend. He was a friend's roommate.'

'And he was a meth dealer?'

'No, a pot dealer. But it's not a healthy lifestyle.'

'Yes,' I said, making one of my doomed attempts to sound clever. 'For one thing the phone is always ringing.'

'Well, he had a cell phone.' Of course he had a cell phone that could be turned to noninterruptive Silent mode. I was showing my age, thinking back to my twenties, to the 1980s, when drug dealers had a single land line that was engaged the whole time and rang again the moment a client hung up.

'I was living in Kirkland, Washington, working for Domino's. The people I was living with weren't paying rent so we got kicked out of our place. We were buying drugs instead of paying rent. It was nice working at Domino's because we could make our own dinner but it was not a good life.'

I almost quipped, 'Handy for when you get the munchies' but thought better of it. Instead I asked her about how and when she'd gotten into drugs in the first place.

'I graduated high school and got in with the wrong crowd.

Lots of drinking and smoking. My friends and I like to drive. There was a lot of drunk driving. Smoking while driving.'

Sonia had grown up in Seattle, Washington. In some ways it was perfectly normal—and not a great cause for alarm—that, as a teenager, she liked drinking and smoking pot. That, after all, is what teenagers *do*. It's when you throw driving into the mix that things swerve off somewhere potentially and easily lethal.

'Anyway, I had to get a waiver to come in because I had smoked pot and because it was on my record. The recruiter was like, "You only smoked pot three times . . ." And in my mind that meant "in one day" but I didn't complete the sentence.'

We all laughed. It was like a moment of shared and hilarious empathy in an NA session where you look back at the good times on drugs and they seem so good you wonder if they might even have been the best times, especially after the second time you had your stomach pumped and ended up in rehab, the time before last.

'I got busted before I joined the Navy. That was the whole reason I joined. My parents paid it off on condition that I went into the Navy.'

'Were they in the military?'

'They were both in the military, yes.' I liked this style of answering a question: not simply 'yes' or 'no', but repeating the question as a declarative affirmation.

'So they were glad that you went into the Navy?'

'They were happy that I joined. They weren't happy that I got into trouble after I joined.'

'That figures,' I said, happy with the way that these little Americanisms came so naturally to me on the boat. 'And when you joined, how did you find boot camp? A jolt to the system presumably.'

'The yelling didn't bother me. The yelling was just stupid. I didn't like the PT and getting up early.' Of course she didn't like getting up early. Getting up early is not what stoners do. Sonia, it had become obvious in the course of our conversation, was extremely easygoing. And that, it turned out, was the problem.

'I'm a follower. Peer pressure's a bitch for me. It just happened the group that I got into did drugs. So I did too.' And now she was in the Navy where being a follower was a good thing—if the things you followed were orders.

Once Sonia had been on restriction and decided to get serious about the Navy she realized she didn't like the way she felt smoking pot. This was part of the big turnaround in her life but take a few things out of the mix (driving, Navy, trouble) and the trajectory described was less dramatic and not at all unusual—almost universal in fact. Though regularly cited, the Manichean jail-or-dead alternatives are often accompanied by some variant of a third: just growing out of . . . Most everybody likes smoking pot for a while and then gradually most everybody doesn't. Or at least they realize that they like *not* being stoned more than they like being stoned. Seen like that Sonia's early life was not an aberration but exemplary: the perfect illustration of *a phase*.

Sonia's voice was giving out but it had been fun talking to her. She was committed to the Navy as a career even if the fit was not absolute. It had made her life better but it hadn't reconfigured her personality and the potentialities she contained to the extent that it had with some people I spoke to. Often a life other than the Navy seemed inconceivable to people in it; or rather *they* seemed inconceivable outside of *it*. Only a small imaginative move sideways was necessary to sense that what seemed—what *was*—thoroughly impressive in uniform could be somewhat limiting and limited outside of it. Sonia retained, even if only through that giggle, the disruptive and unruly potential for a life that was not subject to routine, discipline and orders. Which made her willingness to abide by these standards and rules even more admirable. I asked how old she was, and what her plans were for the future.

'I'm twenty-eight now,' she said. 'I'd like to stay in to do my full twenty. Retire here as chief.'

She was sounding really throaty now, not surprisingly, after all this talking, so I asked just one more question. What about her ex-husband. Did she know what he was up to?

'Last I heard he was working in a tattoo parlour.'

This elicited another round of giggles—an acknowledgment that life's absurdities do not prevent it sometimes acquiring the formal perfection of a sonata—that subsided into a major coughing bout on Sonia's part, the kind of coughing fit you get after you've just taken a hit on a gravity bong.

A sense of purpose and order—even, I am tempted to say, of narrative—was emerging, unbidden, from my time in the carrier—courtesy of Paul, with whom I had established a relationship of easygoing camaraderie. Having seen a former drug user, he asked, was I interested in seeing a drug counsellor? It seemed an excellent idea so we stopped by her office and made an appointment for the next day.

17

The ready rooms of all of the squadrons started out the same way: rows of wide seats lined up to face a whiteboard and TV, giving them the look of business-class cabins on airliners, before the advent of sleeper beds. Like all squadrons on the boat, the VFA-15 (Valions) had taken this template and customized it as extensively as possible. They'd re-tiled the floor in their colours and with their yellow lion insignia. They'd rigged up a hefty sound system so they could play Boston, Linkin Park and a band that sounded like a cheesy version of Slayer. They also had a bar football table, a couch and a popcorn machine.

'You've got it nice in here,' I said to the duty officer—who doubled as DJ and chose the evening's movie on the TV— behind his bank of computer screens.

'Yep, if we had a keg, it'd be perfect,' he said. They didn't have a keg, but they did have bottled beer. Nonalcoholic, of course, but just the action of opening the bottle, chucking the top into the trash and taking a few pulls of this cold, beer-coloured drink felt good. I found myself thinking of pilots in Kent during the Battle of Britain: pissing it up in evening-long sessions at the Dog and Duck and scrambling for their Spitfires the next morning, the remains of hangovers still parching up good parts of their brains. I'd have loved it there then and I was loving it here now, joshing around, playing bar football, eating popcorn and rocking out to Boston—embellished, from time to time, with a bit of low-intensity air guitar from one of the guys.

When we'd finished playing bar football—jeez, I'd forgotten how tough that game was on the lower back—I wandered over to a section of the wall devoted to photos of the guys'

The USS *George H. W. Bush* (right) as seen from
a search-and-rescue helicopter

Landing signal officers watching jets taking off.
Author is second from the right.

Member of the crash-and-salvage crew
on the flight deck

The FOD (foreign object debris) walk

ABOVE: Male berthing area at night
BELOW: The hangar deck at dusk

ABOVE: The Carrier Control Approach room
BELOW: Maintaining aircraft in the hangar

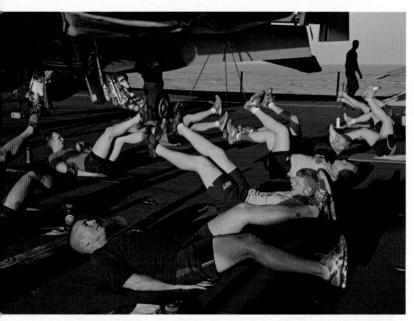

Keep-fit session in the hangar deck

Helicopter co-pilot Theresa Parisi with HSC Trident Group

Jets parked on the flight deck

Jets being moved into parking places at night

Radar surveillance aircraft coming in to land

Walkway at night

wives, girlfriends and kids, all sent recently with nice messages and annotations. There was a picture of all the wives and girlfriends together, back in Norfolk, Virginia, dressed up on a mid-deployment dinner, paid for by the men. It would be dishonest if I did not remark (in the privacy of these pages, I mean; at the time I kept the thought to myself) that some of the Wags were nice-looking, smoking hot, frankly, though that was not the point of the wall. It was a lovely and wholesome thing, the wall. Everything about it was great but I wondered if one of the guys in the squadron didn't have a girlfriend, how the wall made him feel, if it left him feeling lonesome and marooned. Except, looking at the wall and doing a quick calculation it didn't seem that there were any pilots left over (and therefore out). Not everyone had kids but everyone had a sweetheart—and all of these sweethearts were women. The same, statistically, could not have held good for the boat as a whole. Race did not seem an issue on the boat. Having women on board had turned out to be one of the big nonissues. And now legislation had been passed which meant you could be openly gay, getting rid of the earlier code of "Don't Ask, Don't Tell."*

---

*For the record, I asked but no one told. No one responded to my request to speak to someone who was openly gay (and no one mentioned being homosexual in the course of conversations about other stuff). Newell's explanation was that this too was a nonissue so that in relation to three of the big areas of potential intolerance and bigotry the Navy was just about as advanced as any other institution on earth. Except there was, surely, a degree of friction or incompatibility between the evangelical Christian right and the gospel of freedom of sexual expression. Also, in reference to race and gender you don't have to come out as black or female; there is merely the unalterable fact (within reason) of your physical condition. Whereas declaring your sexual orientation was a disclosure of your inner being, of your psychological life. So people might have decided that it was better to just keep quiet about something in a world where plenty of other stuff was kept quiet in the interest of the smooth running of the ship and keeping human relations as uncomplicating as possible. Especially since everything about sex—which meant, principally, going without it—was left unsaid. (There was, of course, another possibility: the fact that no one wanted to speak to me—or, more accurately, that no one wanted to take the time out of their

There was no reluctance, however, to tell and talk about the difference between flying solo and flying two-seater planes.

'Two-man planes are a pilot and a piece of self-loading baggage,' said one of the pilots (call sign 'Disney') as I was hurrying out of the door. I wanted him to expand on this but another pilot (call sign 'Lurch') was taking me up to Vulture's Row to watch the launch and recovery through his night-vision goggles.

I'd been up there—a catwalk high up in the island—once before, in daylight, and it *was* like being a vulture perched on a telegraph wire, waiting to see what happened to the other birds. You didn't have to wear a cranial, just earplugs. I could hear the voice of the Air Boss but, with my earplugs in, could not make out what he was saying. It gave his orders the disembodied quality of the muezzin in a minaret, calling the faithful to prayer.

Even without NV it was a lovely night: moon tilted over on its back, streaks of cloud, sea glittering, oil wells burning orange in the distance, jets roaring off the deck. In the darkness the violence of flight ops was drastically intensified. The jet blast was a solid core of flame burning with such ferocity and force that it seemed the Jet Blast Deflector would melt like reinforced chocolate.

Lurch handed me the goggles. I put them on and entered the NV trance. It took no getting used to. I could see everything on deck: the ground crew scurrying around and lounging, the machinery sharp-edged and unmistakable. All green, of course, green punctuated by lots of white, in just the way NV is presented in the movies but a *lot* clearer. (I wasn't looking at the night-world through the kind of goggles you could pick up in an Army and Navy surplus store or from an ad in the back of *Soldier of Fortune;* this, I'm guessing, was the best NV money could buy, probably the kind of NV money *couldn't* buy.)

already busy days to talk to me about being gay—did not mean they weren't willing to tell friends or people in their dorms.)

After a pilot had landed, he parked the plane and climbed down the step-ladder to greet the members of the flight-deck crew who'd been responsible for his plane. They all huddled round. He fist-bumped each of them. The last thing he did, before disappearing below deck, was to walk to the front of his plane and pat it on the nose, as if it were a horse.

The sea was a prairie of glitter-green. Moon and oil well acquired circles of white light around them. Up overhead—where before there was almost nothing—was a multitude of stars, unimaginably dense, more light than sky, more star than not-star.

18

The following morning signalled the start of a gradual improvement in where and what I ate. Instead of eating breakfast in the Ward Room we upgraded to the Flag Mess. Now this was more like it. The table was covered in a crisp white cloth, places had been set and waiters took your orders—or at least you ringed the things you wanted on a slip of paper and they took away the paper and returned with your food. Decent coffee and tea too. The downside was that I had never been more nervous about etiquette in my adult life.

There were sixteen people round the table, in flying suits and a variety of uniforms, all of them buttering toast and tucking in to eggs. It was a highly persuasive answer to the Taliban, this breakfast: fourteen men and two women, one of whom, seated at the head of the table, was Rear Admiral Nora Tyson. Five thousand people on the boat and she outranked them all. I say that but perhaps the hierarchy was complicated by the Captain's proprietorial command of the ship itself. Although she outranked him in the *Navy* it was still his *boat;* did tradition decree that while she was here she was sort of his guest and deferred to him, could not just come on board and say, 'Set a course for Abadan, we're gonna kick some Iranian butt'?

My omelette arrived and I started to relax, partly because it was a rather nice omelette (with peppers, onions and tomatoes). Newell and I were way down the table; the place to my right had been vacant when we arrived but was now taken by someone whose name and rank I failed (as usual) to register. He seemed to tick off every possible option on the menu (those are the things I *do* register) before offering the most succinct argument for the effectiveness of carriers that I had yet heard.

'We can turn up anywhere and wreak destruction twenty-four hours a day,' he said. But this, it turned out, was not the start of a chest-thumping advert for American sea power. 'People know all about our ability to rain steel on their heads,' he went on. 'They've had that on TV for twenty years straight. But in the event of natural disasters, when the ability of a state or city to function has been destroyed we can provide continuity of operations. That's what the USS *Reagan* did, diverting to Japan after the tsunami hit.'

There was, of course, an acronym for this: MOOTW (Military Operations Other Than War). I was about to reprise my AIE joke but the admiral was taking her leave of the table and we all stood up. She was in her late forties, I guessed (everyone in a senior position looked like they were in their late forties), and was wearing a flying suit. Paul introduced me as she walked past. She was an admiral in the US Navy, from Memphis, Tennessee, and she made me feel as though we'd just bumped into each other on Main Street, that she had nothing particularly pressing to do, would actually have chatted quite happily but didn't want to take up *my* time. She asked if everyone was looking after me OK, asked about my books—she was an English major!—and then left the room to go about the not undemanding business of running the Carrier Strike Group. I had addressed her as 'Admiral' throughout our conversation but was not sure if this was correct.

'Either that or "ma'am" is alright,' said Paul. We had sat down, were working on our omelettes again.

'She was so not intimidating it would be easy just to slip into calling her Nora,' I said. 'What would happen if I'd done that?'

'I'm not sure.'

'What would happen if you did that?'

'If *I* called her Nora? Everything would come to a halt,' he said. 'Including my career.'

19

I wanted to speak again with Disney. I'd taken him as the embodiment of a type sketched by Diane Ackerman in her book about flying, *On Extended Wings:* 'Then aviation went through a military phase, out of which we still haven't evolved. The sky was no longer a mystery, but an invisible nation, territory to be tamed; and planes were just machines, as the people who flew them should be: efficient, cool, stoic, strategic, regular guys, no namby-pambies, who imposed their will on lesser mortals, and knew that, even though the meek might inherit the earth, the strong would inherit the meek.' When we met up again, however, Disney's shaven-headed confidence had turned to tact and diplomacy—to the extent that he asked me not to print the explanation for his call sign. And the earlier crack about two-seater planes was just good-natured ribbing, he said.

'But the thing about solo flying is that your mistakes are your own,' he explained. 'You're as good as you're gonna be on that day. It's just you, on your own in the office, with the best view on the planet.'

'D'you actually get time to look around?'

'When we were taking off from the Indian Ocean into Afghanistan, it was an hour and ten minutes driving up the boulevard as we called it. There was plenty of time to look around then.'

I'd heard that during eventless flying time like that pilots sometimes plugged in their iPods and rocked out in the stratosphere. Disney was unable to confirm or deny such stories, but he did speak of the routine of flying in terms that I would hear several times more in the course of my stay.

'You're flying a video game. You're a weapons and sensors operator more than you're a pilot. The plane is easy to fly. Flies itself almost.' And then, with no change at all in his low slow drawl, he began to talk about a different order of experience. 'You're flying at night, on a gorgeous, clear night. At thirty thousand feet, with the night-vision goggles on, it's like flying through space. You see stars that you never thought you'd see before. Especially if you're over water—that's like flying in deep space.'

So there it was, still intact despite the technological advances and laconic delivery: the lyricism of night flight as first and famously evoked by Saint-Exupéry. It was as if he had revealed something intimate to me, the experience that was at the core of his being: a realm of poetry accessible only to those whose world-view is based on technology, knowledge and calculation rather than wide-eyed wonder. Something similar had happened a couple of nights earlier when I'd been sitting with the Captain and his friends as they smoked their cigars. Amid the talk of service and the fun of flying the Captain had suddenly spoken of how 'with no light pollution, on a night when there's no haze, you can see the majesty of the Milky Way.' And Disney, the kid who'd excelled at video games, for whom it all came down to hand-eye coordination, on keeping an eye on the dials and switches and the data, was having the transcendent experience craved by mystics, shamans, seekers and acidheads.

His evocation of the stars reminded me of a moment in Maurice Herzog's mountaineering classic *Annapurna*. Herzog and his companion Louis Lachenal have conquered the summit but the triumph brings them—and two other members of the expedition who had come to their rescue—to the edge of death as they struggle, snow-blind, shattered, frost-bitten, down the mountain. 'The sky was blue—the deep blue of extreme altitude, so dark that one can almost see the stars.' A few moments later they are engulfed in an avalanche. The privileged glimpse of stars is—as Saint-Exupéry repeatedly and rather grandiloquently insists—underwritten by the inherent danger of the enterprise, the daily possibility of dying: 'the final smash-up,' as he called it in *Wind, Sand and Stars*.

'Have you ever had to eject?' I asked Disney, wondering, too late, if such a question broke a taboo, tempted fate.

'I have not.'

'Ever got close?'

'I guess it depends on your definition of close. But I, uh, managed to salvage the situation well before I reached an envelope where I had to think about getting out.'

Envelope! Love it! We'd been talking a few minutes earlier about the beauty of flying at night, as though through deep space, and now we were back within the linguistic envelope of the pilot's routinely laconic argot. And the downside of flying at night, Disney reminded me, was that you often had to land at night too.

'Nights like these where there's a moon out so you can see what's going on—that's less stressful. But a dark night with terrible weather, low cloud, the boat pitching and you can't see it till the last seconds—that is a terrifying experience. You have instruments telling you what's going on but it's just a postage stamp of a boat down there. Even with all the technology we're still very visual and what you *can't* see terrifies you. You'll land and have trouble getting out of the aircraft because your legs are shaking so much and you're like, *What in the hell am I doing this for? That was just stupid.*'

'How about taking off at night? Is that more straightforward?'

'In some ways I hate a night catapult shot more than I hate a night landing. You sit there, they dim the lights down but your eyes take time to adjust. They shoot you off the front end and on a dark night you've got no visual reference, no idea where the horizon is. It's like getting shot into a black hole. You only have your instruments to trust. On the way down, even on a dark night, you can often see the lights of the ship out in front of you. But when you get shot off Catapult One, the edge lights go and you're in the dark. So you climb, get your night vision on, try to figure out what's going on.'

The odd thing about this was that Disney seemed completely unfazed by what he was saying. Routine, lyricism, terror—all of it was recounted in the same slow, unexcited drawl.

Everything about taking off and landing from a carrier had gotten safer but Disney said something I would hear elsewhere on the carrier. 'A lot of our lessons are written in blood. It's not necessarily a dangerous business, just terribly unforgiving of mistakes.'

20

When we had stopped by to arrange a time for a meeting with the drug counsellor she was wearing a blue T-shirt, and I had glimpsed part of what was evidently a large tattoo on her upper arm. She was in uniform now and the tatt was concealed. To make room for Newell and me, she had to retreat to the far side of her office and sit right under a gun-metal shelf. I worried that she might bang her head when she stood up—it is not only the tall who are at risk.

'A little while back, I gather, drugs were a big problem in the Navy,' I said in a warm-up sort of way.

'Still is,' she said, needing no warm-up at all.

'Oh really? Tell me about that.'

'For some reason now people like to create or just make stuff up for addiction. The new thing is a bath salt—'

'A what?'

'Bath salt. They inhale it. And then of course you've got the whole inhaling sewage to git the high.'

'What?'

'Yes. Why? I don't know why. But they do. And then you've got the classic computer cleaners: inhale it. Pen markers. Git the high. But the biggest thing now is the spice. The spice is a fake marijuana really. I heard about the spice back when I was a counsellor in Japan. It was legal. They were selling it like if you go to a clothing store. Now, with the spice it's rampant because they can't really test for it.'

I was learning a great deal in a very short space of time, all of it entirely new to me, much of it confusing. It was the conversational equivalent of a catapult launch from the flight deck at night: instead of taxiing along the runway, you are just shot off into the darkness, trying to get your bearings.

'Can we go back a paragraph or two?' I said. 'I've not heard of bath salts.* And I've certainly never heard of people getting high on sewage. I mean what part of the sewage process—'

'I couldn't even tell you. I don't have that research. Bath salts though, I do have a paper about that. They contain it in a bag and they just kind of inhale it. I don't know what the process is.'

'What's the high like?'

'I have no idea, sir.'

'You mention sewage, but you don't know anything about it?'

'It's more high schoolers and teenagers that are experimenting on sewage.'

'Just so I'm clear, sewage addiction or sewage abuse—whatever you want to call it—is or is not a problem in the Navy?'

'Definitely not.'

'Ah.' I'd been worried that she might bash her head at the end of our conversation. I wondered now if she had banged it before I came in. Or, looked at another way, she had a highly developed kind of negative capability, was able to bear two completely contradictory ideas in that head of hers without any sense of their cancelling each other out.

'More of our problem in the Navy is probably the spice, because it's not detected,' she continued. 'But it gives you the equal amount of high that marijuana would give.'

'Let's go back to the period when drugs were much more prevalent in the Navy,' I said, re-crossing my legs like a chat-

---

* This was in October 2011. By June the following year everyone had heard of the effects of bath salts, courtesy of Rudy Eugene, who, while under the influence of the substance, chewed off the face of a homeless man, Ronald Poppo, before being shot dead by police in Florida. Or so it was widely reported at the time. The autopsy revealed no trace of bath salts in Eugene's body, but it is hard to see how the drug will ever recover from this catastrophic piece of adverse publicity.

show host about to get to the dank heart of the matter. 'When was the peak time of drug use in the Navy?'

'I don't think there was a peak time. I think it was pretty constant. I mean probably two years ago when they found out about spice, that was the biggest news we ever got, when the spice came out.'

'How about back in the sixties and seventies in Vietnam? Soldiers came back from Vietnam with heroin problems. And there was a lot of grass too. Would there have been a similar thing going on in the Navy at that time?'

'Hmm. I wouldn't compare it to, like, past wars. Current use for drugs is a man will go to Iraq and Afghanistan and come back with post-traumatic stress disorder and the only way they can cope is drugs.'

'Which drugs would they use for that?'

'A lot of cocaine and a lot of marijuana.'

This came as a surprise. I'd heard that there had been some success using Ecstasy to treat PTSD. That made total sense: before it became a rave drug Ecstasy was used in marriage counselling. But coke? Surely, that was not going to help you out if you had PTSD.

'It's not,' she said. 'But for some reason it's very accessible.'

'Do people have addiction problems with other illegal drugs like that—like coke and marijuana?'

'Not illegal drugs necessarily because by the time they get in trouble I don't see them. They're separated from the Navy.'

'Then I'm slightly confused,' I said. 'What exactly are you treating people for?'

'Alcohol.'

Ah, good old alcohol. Always the eventual winner. We went on to discuss the problems of drinking, of young people getting drunk when the ship was at port. In a way I couldn't see what the problem was: young people want to go out and drink a gallon of beer. Especially if they've been on a dry ship for seven months. What could be more normal than that?

'As for drugs,' I said. 'You started by saying it was a huge problem in the Navy. But everything you've said makes me think it's not. Especially compared to kids of the same age in college.'

'As a Navy society, drugs have been more rampant because of the spice. Versus the civilian world of course they've always had that problem but in Navy life it's been huge now because of PTSD, spice, bath salts addiction. But yes, comparing it with civilian life it's not comparable.'

'Sure you're not going to give me the dope on the sewage scene on ship?'

'I don't really know about that. Seems teenage kids have a bag of shit and inhale it. Why? Guess there's the methane.'

'Must be the ultimate cheap high. Though the high sounds incredibly like a low.'

'They call it the bowel bong,' quipped Newell, joining in.

'Imagine the hangover,' I said. 'I mean, most drugs make you feel like shit the *next* day.'

I thanked her for her time, cautioned her again about banging her head as she stood up, and we said our goodbyes. It had been a strange conversation, reminiscent, in some ways, of the ones you have when you're young and getting stoned with friends, the whole thing flowing along with barely a pause, frequently hilarious but often, for quite long stretches, making no sense at all. Drugwise, there was a huge problem—and there was no problem. Lots of people wanted to git the high—were willing to do anything to git the high—but it seemed like hardly anyone was actually gittin' the high.

Listening to the tape in my rack that night, after Lights Out, I thought the conversation seemed, if anything, even more bizarre once it had been freed from the tacit laws and patterns that shape face-to-face conversation. I started saying the phrase 'git the high' and its variant, 'gittin' the high', over and over, at first chuckling happily to myself and then laughing out loud, gittin' the high just from saying 'gittin' the high'. If I'd had the equipment and ability I'd have gone back in time and used my computer to build a big dance track—a choon, as they probably don't say anymore—around those samples, 'git the high' and 'gittin' the high'. From Ibiza to Detroit and London it would have eschewed the elevating pseudo-spiritual bollocks of Josh Wink's 'Higher State of Consciousness' in favour of straight-ahead hedonism; it would have become a house classic, available in multiple remixes, all climaxing repeatedly with the diagnosis and warning turned on its head, building to that anthemic, gospel-tinged admonition: 'G . . . G . . . G . . . Git-the . . . . Git-the . . . Git-the . . . ' until, finally, inevitably, it arrives, the raise-your-hand-in-the-air, eyes-the-size-of-night-vision-planets release: 'GIT THE HIGH!'

21

Imagine this: you're sitting in that boring old thing a commercial airliner. You say 'hi' to the attractive woman—early thirties, blonde—next to you. When dinner arrives you get talking, ask what she does. She might say she's in the Navy. Expecting the next answer to be 'I'm in avionics' or 'radar'—or, if you are thoroughly unreconstructed, 'I work in the hair salon'—you ask what exactly she does. Or, in response to that opening question, she might reply, 'I'm a pilot,' in which case you follow up with 'What kind of pilot?' Either way, assuming she's in the mood to chat, she will at some point concede the truth: I'm a fighter pilot, flying F-18s, off a carrier.

I was not in the position of that excited passenger: I was in the still more fortunate position of talking to Jax (her call sign) in the ready room of her squadron. In the imagined civilian context of the preceding paragraph her hair was blonde; here, it seemed the same colour as her flying suit. The first thing to ask was how she came by her call sign.

'When you land the jet too hard you get a maintenance code of 904. And you have to put the jet up on jacks every time you land too hard. The area code for Jacksonville is 904. In my first squadron I didn't like to go around so I made sure to land even if it broke the jet. It did not win me many friends on the maintenance crew but it got me a call sign.'

'You didn't take your bolter like a man?' said Newell.

'I did not. I took my landing like a woman.'

Aside from the fact that she was a woman flying jets—one of a handful of women on the carrier to be flying and the only one flying solo—her story conformed closely to that of others except in one important particular: *Top Gun* played no part in making her want to become a pilot. She grew up in Colorado. Her father was an intelligence officer in the Air Force. The Navy paid her college fees—at Northwestern University in Chicago. After a year she chose aviation, became a pilot and ended up here, in the ready room, talking to me.

I'd asked her to tell me her story briefly; I wasn't expecting it to be *that* brief. During all her training, for instance, did she encounter any kind of resistance to the idea of a woman entering this high citadel of manliness?

'All of us have had an experience of old-style chauvinism. But throughout flight school it was always very fair. And still is. If I'm not flying the ball well everyone knows.'

'Flying the ball?'

'The landing lens. There's a single light source in the middle that we call the ball and you reference it to a line of green lights. When you're high, the ball is above the datums; if you're low it's below the datums. You try to centre the ball. Based on what your power is the ball will actually move.'

'So there's nothing to it really?'

'Not really.'

We have an idea of the fighter pilot as swaggering, macho, thrust forward into the world by the G-force—strictly speaking that should be negative G—of implacable self-belief. Jax was as nice as pie. Couldn't have been nicer or less swaggering but, by commenting on the 'level of arrogance that is needed and then bred into you' by training and profession, she tacitly admitted to a determination and fixity of purpose below that nice-as-possible manner. (Would it make sense to say that she had an *inner* swagger? Is such a thing even conceivable?) Any residue of that old chauvinism must have put more challenges in her way than confronted a male of similar age and equivalent abilities. It wasn't possible, surely, that she'd ended up in a position that so many others aspired to—at the very tip of the frequently cited spear—without having *wanted* to get there more than anyone else? Or were the Navy's meritocratic procedures of selection and advancement so refined that someone of outstanding natural talent could end up flying jets without the aid of rocket-booster ambition?

Either way, it seemed, the Navy was not capable of hanging on to Jax. She'd been in for twelve years but was getting out. The Navy was keen to keep her—understandably, since it had invested a phenomenal amount of money in developing her skills, experience and expertise—but her mind was made up. (I didn't ask if she was in a relationship, but at her age the question of children was on the horizon. It's one thing to be a mother with a three-year-old kid at home, on deployment as a mechanic; quite another to be away for seven months flying combat ops.) So, what was she going to do when she got out?

'Environmental research.'

'On the damage done by tearing through the atmosphere supersonically?'

'My degree was in environmental science,' she added, but you did not need a degree to see that she had wreaked a disproportionate amount of ecological havoc for one so young. 'I have a lot of bad karma that I need to work out,' she said, joking and not joking.

As we were walking back to our rooms Paul bumped into someone he knew—he was *always* bumping into people he knew—who said that, if we were interested, this would be a good time to take a look at one of the male berthing areas. (We'd been meaning to do this for several days but it had never quite worked out.)

The dorm was illuminated by soft red light that was quite cosy: homely even, in a massive sort of way. We walked down the corridors between six-packs (three-tier bunks stacked either side of a partition). We'd had our royal-visitors interlude back in the bakery; now we were having a Whitman walk-through. Each rack had a curtain to pull along its length for privacy. Most people were racked out already, it seemed, either sleeping or listening to music on their iPods; a few were getting ready to turn in; a handful were still at computer terminals or chatting quietly.

'How many people here?' I whispered as we were leaving.

'Two hundred and eighteen men, rank of E-6 and below.'

'Jeez, that's a lot of guys.'

'Yep, that's a lotta attitudes back there,' said our guide as we exited the berth. Not surprisingly, these attitudes manifested themselves mainly as fart, deodorant and aftershave: smell and anti-smell—thesis and antithesis—creating a synthesis of both.

22

One of the perks of having my own room was the freedom to fart whenever I felt the urge. The disadvantage was that Newell invariably knocked on my door seconds after I'd done so. It was almost as if, by breaking wind, I had summoned him—a faster and more efficient method than calling him on the phone. On this occasion he and the snapper had come to tell me that our visit to Flight Deck Control had been moved forward so we had to get up there right away.

Flight Deck Control was the fiefdom of Lieutenant Commander Ron Rancourt, a man seriously in love with what he did. More in love—if such a thing was possible—than the other people I'd met who were seriously in love with what they did. He had a commanding view of the flight deck from his chair in what he called 'the nerve centre of flight operations'. In front of him was a plexiglass-covered table with a plan of the flight deck, on top of which were little model planes and helicopters, variously adorned with different coloured nuts. It was like a large-scale board game called Carrier Strength or Flight Deck—though Ron referred to it simply as the Ouija board. After all the blinking lights, data streams and illuminated coordinates on plasma screens it was nice seeing this hands-on throwback to the days of the Battle of Britain when WAAFs would broom little cardboard planes around a giant map of our island fortress. Nostalgic feelings were entirely appropriate as it turned out; after this deployment Ron's quaintly efficient board would be replaced by a new electronic system in keeping with the super-tech style of operations elsewhere on the ship. Around the edge of the board, under the glass, were banknotes of various denominations in many different currencies.

Ron's hair was clipped short. He smiled all the time that he was talking. He was engaged totally by our conversation but—such is the absolute concentration demanded by his job—a simple task like talking to me meant he had a good 20 or 30 per cent concentration left over for whatever else was going on. And there was quite a lot else going on. Even by the crowded and busy standards of the boat this was a crowded and busy spot with people coming and going the whole time. One of these was a guy in a red cape and a kind of *Star Wars* outfit, complete with helmet and vizor: part of the Halloween festivities that had earlier included an entirely serious-sounding announcement, over the Main Circuit, that a 'zombie attack' was in progress. Amid the background clatter and distraction of equipment, phones ringing and voices calling out coordinates, Ron enunciated his role with an unerring clarity of purpose. He was responsible for the safety and movement of all the embarked aircraft on board: sixty-six in total.

'When we're launching and recovering aircraft we have to be going into the wind and heading straight. But that's when the ship is most vulnerable. So the shorter we make that launch and recovery window the better. We're always shooting for effectiveness, always shooting for a thirty-minute window from launching the first bird to recovering the last.' (How long would I need to be on the carrier before hearing the planes referred to as birds lost its thrill? How long before I was able to spontaneously use the term myself, for it to come tripping off my tongue as naturally as birds to the trees?) We were, it goes without saying, in one of the lulls outside that window now. Another advantage of this tight window, from the point of view of the rest of the crew, was that the crash and thump of jets landing and taking off was concentrated into bunched periods of hellish noise, rather than a continuous nerve-jarring din. But that din, for Ron, was as soothing as a lullaby—or anti-lullaby, one designed to keep his team awake and in a state of constantly high alert for hours on end. I asked him what kind of shifts he put in.

'Fourteen to sixteen hours every day.'

'Is anyone else able to do your job?'

'I'm the only aircraft handling officer on the ship.'

'What happens when you get sick?' asked the snapper.

'I don't get sick.'

'OK,' I said, taking over, tag-style. 'What happens when you want to watch TV?'

'TV is poison.'

'Ah, OK. But I'm struggling a bit with the maths of your day,' I say. 'Let's say you put in a fifteen-hour day . . .'

'I go to my room, read a bit to unwind and then I have my alarm set at four to go to the gym. At a minimum I try to get five or six hours sleep a night.'

I mentioned that studies had shown—studies, needless to say, which I'd not even seen, let alone read—that after a certain number of hours of work people get less efficient, make more mistakes.

'I get to a point when my train of thought is not as sharp, probably round the fourteen-hour mark.'

I had lost my train of thought somewhere around the fourteen-word mark. So I looked at the miniature planes on the board in front of Ron's chair, decorated with little pins, nuts and other bits and pieces—green, blue, yellow and purple—all symbolizing something about the status of the aircraft, its readiness and its requirements. A purple nut meant the jet needed fuel. A yellow block meant TOD (tail over deck) or TOW (tail over water).

'You see some planes have washers on them,' said Ron. 'Which means . . . ?'

My hand shot up—Me sir! Me sir!—and I called out the answer before the snapper had a chance even to open his mouth. 'It means the plane needs a wash!'

'That's right.' Oh, the bliss of getting answers right, of doing so publicly and being seen to be the cleverest boy in class.

'Do I get one of those bills as a prize?' I said, pointing at the money beneath the glass.

'That comes later,' said Ron. 'Now, what about these planes with a wing nut on them?'

'Something to do with the wing?' snapped the snapper. 'Fold up the wings maybe?'

'You got it,' said Ron. The snapper had equalized, but here's the thing that marks me out as a leader, as SEAL material. I didn't sit there glowering, sulking or licking my wounds. Before Ron asked his next question, before I even knew there was going to be another question, I was looking round the board to see what other symbolic cargo the planes were carrying. So by the time Ron asked the question, about the planes with a little jack on them, I had already—repeat: Alpha, Lima, Romeo, Echo, Alpha, Delta, Yankee, *already*—worked out the answer by reference to intel gained just hours before from Jax, and was able to sing it out before he'd even finished his sentence.

'The aircraft's been jarred on landing and needs to be put on jacks, sir!' I didn't wait for Ron to say, 'Affirmative' or 'Correct', I just held my arms aloft, fists clenched, basking in it. In what? In that raising-the-flag-on-Iwo-Jima, watching-the-Zulus-slink-away-from-Rorke's-Drift glow otherwise known as *V* for victory in a *Q* for quiz.

There was no time to gloat. Ron was continuing his explanation of what went on here. Like Charles in the kitchens he used the first-person possessive when talking about the flight deck, as in 'getting a damaged aircraft off of my flight deck.' This intense personal investment in the site of his expertise was justified on the grounds that he'd been doing it—or working his way towards it from his early days as an enlisted man—for twenty-eight years. For a long time working on a flight deck was regarded as the most dangerous job in the world; now, Ron explained, it was 'the safest most dangerous job in the world.'* At least on his watch it was. In twenty-eight years there'd been no deaths on any of the decks he'd worked.

The birds would soon be launching and recovering. With the tempo and intensity of concentration and activity increasing, the snapper and I would need to leave—but not before another triumph on my part. The money under the glass, round the edges of the table; what was the story behind that?

'A fine paid by any visitor who touches it or puts stuff there.' This had proved a profitable form of taxation. When they were stateside and receiving visitors every day they collected four thousand dollars in a nine-month period—all of it donated to a scholarship programme. I had put my coffee on Ron's Ouija board—but only *after* checking that it was OK to do so!

'That's correct,' he said. 'You had my permission.'

---

*Annie Dillard arrived at a similar conclusion when she became fascinated by a stunt pilot in her book *The Writing Life:* 'I had thought that danger was the safest thing in the world, if you went about it right.'

23

Ron had been so passionate about his job that it was impossible to imagine him not doing it. Or, to put it the other way around, it was impossible to imagine the job being done by anyone other than him. So it came as a surprise when Paul revealed, over dinner, that Ron was 'getting out'. He'd mentioned that he had three daughters who were all being home-schooled by his wife—a task he would now share with her. I wanted to ask him more about his planned voluntary renunciation of high-level, high-stress responsibility in favour of this deep entrenchment in domestic life and education, so we arranged to go back there the following day, right after we got off the bird. That's right, we were going for a spin in a helo (pronounced *heel*-oh): an MH-60R Seahawk.

The helos are first up and last back in any launch and recovery cycle. During flight ops there are always a couple of helos in the air. They patrol the area around the ship in case of attack or, more plausibly, a plane going into what Spitfire pilots used to call the drink. (Possible elision of two distinct idioms, one from *Black Hawk Down*, the other from the Battle of Britain: 'We have a bird in the drink! Repeat: the bird is having a drink!')

We got suited up in float coats and helmets—not cranials, actual solid helmety thingies—and prepared to board. The bird came in to land and chain gangs rushed forward to anchor it. As always happened at moments like these—the interface of man and machine—there was a sudden coming together of the technologically advanced and the extremely basic. Among those rushing forward was a squeegee guy who started wiping down the windshield. It was as though the bird had stopped at a red light and he needed to work his squeegee hustle before the pilot had a chance to decline this unrequested clean. The old crew stepped off and we—a crew of four plus me and the snapper—took their places. We strapped ourselves in—or rather, since my straps were in such a tangle, I had to *be* strapped in, like a lanky toddler being settled for the night. Our feet rested, toughly, on ammo cases. Everywhere were more straps, clips, fixings. Everything could be clipped to, fixed to and detached from everything else. As we were about to take off the ground crew crouched like runners in a middle-distance race about to dash forward again—but they were just bracing themselves against the downdraft.

It didn't feel like take-off. More like a slight wobble caused by the Gulf conveniently lowering itself fifteen feet.* And then we were off and the carrier was beneath us. How big was the carrier? Again, it was impossible to say. From the air it was the only thing around—the only game in town—and therefore of no particular size, relatively speaking.

Condensation dripped from pipes over our heads. There was a constant mist of cold steam blowing from somewhere. We began making the rounds, round and round. It was a bit confusing: why was it only the port side of the carrier that swung reliably into view every ten minutes? Because, it turned out, although we were going round and round we were not going round and round the carrier, just round and round one side of it. The starboard side was patrolled by another helo.

The helos' mission was search and rescue, their motto 'So that others may live'. As co-pilot Theresa Parisi put it, 'In order for us to make a difference somebody else has to have a very bad day.' She was the only female in search and rescue, and she'd got into this line of work because she was told she couldn't.

---

* As per producer Lew Grade's line about his critically panned box-office flop *Raise the Titanic*: 'It would have been cheaper to have lowered the Atlantic.'

Through our headsets she and the pilot started to explain what the bird *could* do but I interrupted with a question that had been troubling me since we boarded. When talking about the—or a—'bird', was one referring to a helo or a plane or both?

'If you're on the ground,' Theresa explained, 'it can mean both, as in "Which bird am I flying in?" But once you're in the air "bird" refers just to rotary aircraft, to helos.'

With that uncertainty cleared up she and the pilot resumed their summary of how the bird could hover at ten feet at ten knots, or fifteen feet while completely stationary. From either of these heights the swimmer can jump into the water. From seventy feet the swimmer can descend on a rope. This is what the crew members want to do: they want to jump the swimmer. I was familiar with the phrase 'jump the shark' but not 'jump the swimmer'. Great expression! After I got back to London I would be walking down the street and suddenly call out, 'Jump the swimmer!' If my wife was with me she would call back, 'Swim the jumper!' and we'd go down the street together shouting out, 'Jump the swimmer!' and 'Swim the jumper!' like a couple of crazy people.

To give us a sense of what jumping the swimmer involved the winch was lowered, with a survival basket attached. If you were lost at sea with sharks taking bites out of your feet it would be lovely to see the bird coming to rescue you like this but, in doing so, the helo turns the sea into a terrifying aquatic inferno as if livid at having to give up one that it had claimed as its own. Your bad day gets abruptly worse right before it gets better. We hung there for a while, gazing down at the rotor-tormented sea, then climbed away.

I had only ever been in a helicopter once before, over a glacier in New Zealand, so it was a real thrill being up in the bird like this—for about twenty minutes. Then we settled into the remainder of a three-hour shift that, for the crew, had become as routine as driving a flying bus in perfect weather with a couple of .50 cals (at least I'm guessing that's what they were) poking out of either side in anticipation of trouble that never looked like coming. Nobody was having a bad day. The swimmer was not going to be jumped—the jump would not be swum—so the crew passed the time just shooting the breeze. I got the impression this is what they did every day, in different permutations, according to who was flying with whom: they flew round and round and chatted. Today they were talking about the Steelers (whose name, I had learned since hearing it on the bridge a few days previously, was spelled like that).

'Yeah, I got a buddy who's a Steelers fan and he's got a Steelers room in his house. You're not allowed to enter the Steelers room if there's not a Steelers game on TV. And you can't go watch a Steelers game unless you have a Steelers jersey on. So he's kind of brainwashed his kids from an early age. It's quite impressive.'

While this monologue was in progress the crew chief on the right side was eating an orange and so, coincidentally, was the rescue swimmer on the left. Both chipped in from time to time with their own thoughts about the Steelers. I enjoyed hearing the relaxed back and forth of chat on my headset though I was often unable to tell who was talking—unless it was Theresa. It was like having voices in your head, thoughts that were not your own. The carrier kept going by. The steady thump of the rotors made it impossible to stay awake. I slumped forward in my harness, voices fading into the clatter of dream. When I lurched awake the voices had moved on to ice hockey and someone was telling the others about a game he'd gone to.

'You know in a football game when a guy goes down the crowd goes all quiet and when he gets up again and they can see he's not hurt too bad they cheer? When this guy went down they started counting him out like a boxer. And when he got up they threw stuff at him.'

I looked out of the side of the bird, down at the carrier—the bird's nest, I suppose. The deck was busy with brightly dressed people strolling in a line that stretched from one side of the boat to the other, as if they were on a tightly organized cruise ship. And then we were past it and there was just the blue ocean and the sky-grabbing thump of rotors again.

24

Right after landing I was back in Flight Deck Control where Ron was presiding over the bustle of activity from his chair—which he promptly vacated and offered to me. I am the kind of person who, if staying with friends, will always take the best seat in the house, the sofa with the best view of the TV or in the middle of the hi-fi's cone of sound. But I had the good sense to decline this offer, not to sit and swing around in Ron's chair like I was Gene Kranz. I just stood near it, taking care not to blow any money by inadvertently touching or putting anything on the Ouija board.

'So,' I said. 'Is this true about you retiring?'

'Absolutely. I've been doing this for twenty-eight years. This is my seventh carrier. I have an absolute passion for being out on the flight deck, moving aircraft and, maybe this sounds too patriotic, doing it for freedom. But yeah, it is coming to an end for me.'

It was the mark of the man that he could say this without a hint of . . . I was going to say 'regret' but I remembered that moment in *Chariots of Fire* when Eric Liddell is asked if he has regrets about dropping out of the race (because he's a devout Christian and won't compete on a Sunday) and he replies, unhesitatingly: 'Regrets yes. Doubts no.' Maybe Ron had neither and that was how he'd got to where he had in life. But what lay ahead for him?

'I have very young children and I feel it's my duty as a dad now to go home and raise my children in a good moral Christian manner.'

'You mean home-schooling?'

'Yes. We want to be the influence on our children. We didn't want the public [i.e., state] schools' playgrounds to influence their character or their values or their morals. Our curriculum is based on Christianity and God. I'm not bashing public school—by no means—but we've gotten so far away from where this country was founded. It was founded on Christianity. The separatists who left England left for a reason, so they could be free and practise Christianity based on God. And we've taken so much of that out because of today's politics. You can't even say the Pledge of Allegiance in schools anymore. My kids do that.'

Ron said this in the same evenly impassioned way that he described the workings on the flight deck. He wasn't saying it in a crazy way at all, but he still sounded a little crazed to me. And the plan seemed preprogrammed to blow up in his face. You don't have to read Edmund Gosse's *Father and Son* to see that this is the kind of upbringing practically guaranteed to turn your sons or daughters into atheists, converts to Islam or just zonked-out acidheads. But—you see, this is the benefit of doubt—maybe it *could* work, maybe these kids would turn out to be upstanding, good Christian folk who would home-school their own kids too . . . And who was I to say there was anything wrong with that? I still felt I should engage with Ron about his idea of what the US was and was meant to be.

'You know, we're here,' I said, without knowing exactly where we were. 'We're I don't know how many miles from Iran. Isn't the essence and greatness of the US—as opposed to a theocracy like Iran over there—that you have freedom of religious belief and practice, including freedom not to believe in anything at all except that freedom?'

'Absolutely.' (A favourite word of Ron's; I had never met anyone who was able to make the word 'absolutely' sound so . . . absolute. When he said 'absolutely' he meant it, absolutely.) 'I totally support that—that's the beauty of the US. The right of free speech, being free. But I think we've gone so far left of that

that we're not seeing everything in an equal manner. We—my wife and I—go by what this country was founded on, what we stood for. It was founded by people from all other nations, black and white, all the different religions. And the fact that we can all come together, that is awesome. But we also need to respect what this country was founded on. I am a firm believer in Jesus Christ as my saviour, and God, and that's what we wanna base our curriculum on.'

Nothing Ron said was surprising. A few years previously I'd read an essay by Christopher Hitchens called 'In Defence of Foxhole Atheists' in which he pointed out that 'unexamined extremist Christian conservatism is the cultural norm in many military circles.' Ron was willing to fight and die for the Constitution, and I, lacking the clarity and argumentative zeal of Hitchens, was not sure about the extent to which his beliefs were at odds with it. What was clear and not at all surprising, however, was that these spiritual beliefs did not exist in an ideological and political vacuum.

'I think we have gone overboard with what government was first designed for,' said Ron. 'The purpose of government was, number one, to protect the country with a strong military—it wasn't all about the free hand-outs. Not to support the people in terms of putting food on the table—that isn't what it was designed for. I have a lot of other opinions about that.'

'About Obama's health-care reforms, for example?' I said.

'I'm outraged,' said Ron, but although he was outraged his voice did not become raised, and he continued to speak with the smile that had animated his face throughout this and our previous conversation. 'Look at my family. I have five brothers and sisters all struggling. Up in New Hampshire, near the Canadian border. Three of them are contractors, working for themselves, building houses. Their medical care is simply when they have an emergency they go to the hospital and pay for it out of their pocket. Now they're gonna be forced to get health care and if they don't it will be imposed on them, they will have a fine or even go to jail. You're forcing people to do things now. This is a free country. You have choices. You have a choice to get an education or not. You have a choice to get a job or not. But to be forced to get health care . . .'

There was quite a lot to disagree with. Like the line about getting an education or not. A lot of people joined the Navy precisely because they *couldn't* choose—couldn't afford—to go to college. So they were *obliged* to choose the Navy. And while Obama's health-care reforms provoked intense indignation among other crew members I spoke with, one of the Navy's inducements to join is excellent medical care for people otherwise unable to afford it. I am not a confident debater—and I was not there to debate anyway. So I asked Ron about the next phase of his life, if he thought he'd have trouble adjusting from the all-consuming intensity of his current . . . job? The word hardly did justice to how he spent his days.

'My whole life I have had a title. I've always been a flight-deck guy. I'm an officer. I have a rank. I'm the aircraft handling officer. When I retire that's all gone. And I've been doing this fast-paced high-excitement job. Yeah, so I have a big challenge ahead of me and I trust that the Lord has a plan for me. I hope he does.'

Our talk came to an end shortly after that—the birds would soon be launched and recovered—leaving me to reflect on my meeting with Ron. He was patently a good man, a man you could trust with your life, your wife, your car, the defence of your country—anything—but a little frightening nonetheless. Ron was the nearest thing to a zealot I had ever met, but my time on the ship meant I was encountering an America I had not come across before, an aquatic version of the Midwest and the Bible Belt South. In spite of what the Bish had said when he showed us round the chapel, it was hard to resist the conclusion that this was an intensely religious ship, with its fair share of people who, by my standards, were religious nuts. Take Ensign Newell, whose only bit of weirdness, you might have thought, was his fanatical devotion to that moustache of his. When I mentioned to him that I thought Ron was a zealot Paul announced that he was one too! Paul had devoted his life to Christ—and was a spectacular advert for doing so. He was a great guy, super-efficient at everything he did, always stepping up to the plate when I couldn't think of any questions to ask during interviews, unfailingly providing extra information about anything at all that I needed explained. And then, whenever we were on our own, we'd just be bantering back and forth in the way that guys do, talking about women (though not in the way most guys do: 'God's most beautiful creation' was Paul's preferred appellation). Still, it took a while before I could broach the subject of something he did before every meal: quickly and silently lowering his face to within a few inches of the plate with his hands either side of his head as though in a state of complete despair.

'I can relate to that,' I said one lunch-time. 'I feel the same way about the food myself. But now I know you better, I realize that you're asking God for the strength to face the ordeal of eating this slop.'

'I'm actually praying for your atheist's soul,' he said.

'A fault was reported on that phone line over a hundred years ago,' I said. 'These days you won't even get a dial tone.'

It was fun, joking around like this, but although I was as zealous in my anti-faith as Paul was in his belief I would be lying if I did not confess to a slight chink in my armour of nonbelief. In bed at night I had gone from listening with pleasure to the pre–Lights Out prayer to . . . not joining in, exactly, just concentrating along with it as a way of bringing the day into some kind of focused conclusion. *Heavenly Father . . .*

25

The person explaining the part played by ordnance and showing us around one of the magazines on the boat was Lieutenant Commander Dave Fowler from North Florida, just south of the Alabama state line. He was in his mid-forties, with hair buzzed close up the back and sides (i.e., he had the same haircut as almost all males on the boat who weren't shaven-headed or bald). He'd joined as an enlisted man, made chief petty officer in '96 and was commissioned in 2000.

'Ah've had a blast,' he said.

'So to speak,' I said. The truth is that Dave was *still* having a blast. He seemed like he might explode with efficiency and zeal. He reeled off bomb types and missile names, smart bombs that could be dumbed down and dumb bombs that could be smartened up. Whatever you wanted a bomb for, chances are he could get one to do it. He had bombs that could climb down a chimney like Santa Claus, beam back footage of the contents of your living room and then blow the place to kingdom come, leaving the surrounding neighbourhood shocked but otherwise unscathed. He introduced me to his colleague Jim who had an obvious biological advantage over Dave: shaven-headed and huge, he was actually built like a bomb; didn't work in ordnance, he *was* ordnance. As for Dave, he was a movie star, Jim told me.

'That true, Dave?'

'Well, back in 2000 when Ah was on the USS *Belleau Wood* Den*zel Wash*ington came on board to shoot *Antwone Fisher* and they opened up some of the parts to the active duty that were on board and Ah went up and read for a part and Den*zel* picked me for the chief master-at-arms.'

'Why'd he pick you?'

'Ah think he lahked mah ac*cent*.'

'I bet,' I said, holding my Dictaphone a little closer, to make sure I captured it properly.

'Anyways, they shot it and now Ah know why the movies are so perfect when we see them because they shoot the same scene over and over and over again. We did it so many tahms Ah ended up with three words. "Stand at attention." Ah shot the scene with James Brolin who played the CO. Friend told me Den*zel* got mad because James Brolin kept screwing up his lines so we had to do it over and over. Most of it ended up on the cutting room floor but that friend of mahn said, "You don't realize what you just *did*." "Hell, Ah just shot a little scene for a movie." "No, you had a *major* speaking role in Den*zel Wash*ington's direc*tor*ial deh*but*. There's people out there in Hollywood who would kill to have that oppuh*tun*ity." Ah could be in the Screen Actors Guild if Ah so choosed. That was mah fifteen seconds of fame. Ah've had people come up to me and say, "Are you the guy from that damned *Antwone Fisher* movie?"'

'Great story,' I said. Then, looking crestfallen at my Dictaphone: 'Shit, the tape didn't work. Would you mind saying that over again?'

Bear in mind that my accent was every bit as unusual to Dave as his was to me. To him it was the very sound of uptight Englishness, reinforced by a resolutely unsmiling English face. He looked for a moment as if he really might explode and then there was laughter and shoulder thumping all round. It was a classic long-fuse, delayed-action English gag.

'He got you there!' Jim boomed.

'He really did,' Dave conceded.

Now it was time to get serious and descend into one of the actual magazines—I'd thought that's where we were already but it was just some kind of anteroom. Like potholers of the future, we climbed through hatches only big enough to take a big man down vertical ladders.

'OK,' said Dave when we had completed our descent. 'This is where the rubber meets the road.' How Americans love places where the rubber meets the road! He was right, of course, the rubber met the road here, but this was not the only time and place on the carrier where such a claim was made. The rubber seemed to meet the road all over the ship. But then America *is* the place where the rubber dreams of meeting the road—and vice versa. Certainly the rubber doesn't meet the road with anything like the same frequency or enthusiasm in England. In many ways England is the place where, rubber-and-road-wise, never the twain shall meet.

There were bombs and bomb parts stacked up everywhere. It was an IKEA of munitions—conveniently located not in the outskirts of the ship but in its basement—with everything stacked neatly in parts, ready to be assembled without the aid of wordless instructions, incomprehensible diagrams and missing vital components.

Everything looked like it weighed at least a ton. The sense of order was equal to that of the explosive threat that neatness had been designed to counter. Keep it neat and ordered and lethality can be rendered harmless. Chaos is threat. Mess is danger.

'This is one magazine out of thirty-four,' Dave explained. 'Book says we should be able to eat off the floor of these magazines, so they need to be kept scrupulously clean. We spend a lot of time cleaning and inventorying. We are a hundred per cent accountable for every piece of ordnance we have in here. We're constantly inventorying all the time. Right now we're doing a major re-set in preparation for going home, going back through, inventorying everything. Day check is doing all the inventorying, night check will go through and support what day check needs to get done. As you can see, bombs are packed in there real tight. I've got magazines with missiles and ancillary equipment where you can't get a sheet of paper between two things. So it all needs to get laid out and inventoried.'

I was reminded of those times—they happened once a year—when my dad had to work through the weekend, stocktaking. After he died—this was when I was back from the carrier—we cleared out his drawers and found boxes of staples he'd smuggled out of the workplace and squirreled away at home thirty years previously, in anticipation of some rainy stapling day that never quite came. Dozens of boxes of pencils too.

As Dave talked a number of ratings in red shirts—mag rats as they are known—were manoeuvring bomb parts on trolleys across the room. Some of the shirts had IYAOYAS stencilled on them.

'What does that mean?' I asked.

'The aviation ordnanceman's motto is "Peace Through Power: We Are the Arms of the Fleet,"' Dave said. 'But because of the close-knit camaraderie of the red shirts that is probably more visible than any other rate that's in the Navy someone came up with the slogan IYAOYAS: "If you ain't ordnance you ain't shit."'

Paul said he'd been aware of this camaraderie throughout his time in the Navy. It was acknowledged by everyone.

'Why is that?' I asked.

'Well, look at the environment,' said Dave. 'When you're working with the multitude of live ordnance we got here, if a fire were to break out … Each one of those is a five-hundred-pound weapon, each one of these is two hundred fifty pounds of explosive filler. So one skid … I'm looking at fifteen hundred pounds of explosive filler on one skid.' (The thing I had called a trolley was a skid, clearly.) 'Once that goes up and goes boom it's a chain reaction—this thing's gonna go off like a Roman candle.' This seemed to understate things. A Roman candle was, by comparison, harmless, decorative. 'That's the way we bond together. Everybody's got to look out for one another. We can't do anything in here by ourselves. We don't even enter a magazine by ourselves. Everything is done in a minimum group of two. Normally we're in groups of five or seven. Our weapons-builds go anywhere from seven to ten personnel working together.'

Those were the day-to-day practicalities. The underlying thing, he said, 'is that the rules we live by are written in blood.'

Disney, the embodiment of the fighter pilot's ethos of solitary glory, had said the same thing. These claims to a heritage of blood competed with but did not cancel each other out. The communal spirit of the boat was fostered by each department taking specific pride in its unique contribution. The closer this contribution came to danger and the unleashing of violence, the more pronounced the pride became. It was all about how close you were to the tip of the spear, to the tip of the tip.

Jim picked up where Dave had left off, further embellishing the IYAOYAS creed.

'If a plane's not carrying ordnance it's a dang pleasure craft. If we didn't have ordnance this boat would just be a floating platform for a bunch of fancy, overpaid video guys putting on an air show.'

There was even competition within your group to express derision of rivals—as a way of confirming your loyalty to your peer group. 'If it's a two-seater it's just someone in the back seat going "Wheeee . . . !"' Ah, so there was agreement with Disney on that score.

'And if it's a single-seater without ordnance it's just another unscheduled airline,' said Jim, breaking off this momentary alliance with the pilots.

'You can fly fast and track somebody. But when you've flown fast and tracked them what you gonna do then?' asked Dave.

'You're gonna blow the living shit out of them!' I said, getting the hang of things.

'*If* you got ordnance,' boomed Dave and Jim together.

26

On the carrier, aside from working out there is not a lot to do after work. That expression 'after work' is a little misleading in any case since, for many crew members, there is no such thing. Fourteen-hour days are not unusual. And some of the sailors spend their spare time studying—which is what students call work. Then there's the problem of *where* to go after work in a place that is essentially a giant workplace. Films are shown most nights on the big TV screens in the mess halls but Halloween had had a horrible effect on the scheduling:

Friday, October 28th: *The Texas Chainsaw Massacre*
Saturday, October 29th: *The Exorcist*
Sunday, October 30th: *Halloween*

Perhaps now, with Halloween out of the way, we'd move on to better films. Naturally, I would like to have guest-curated the films shown on the boat but no one asked me to get involved. Perhaps they feared an inappropriate programme of Tarkovsky and Antonioni when in fact I would have chosen films with a nautical theme, a special season of British Second World War films called something like 'The War at Sea: A Tribute to John Mills'. Or a week of submarine films ... But then it's possible that, after six months at sea, they'd already screened every maritime film ever made, had lost track of the number of times they'd sat through *Das Boot, Master and Commander, The Poseidon Adventure, Titanic* ...

Apart from watching movies, people in the mess halls, most evenings, were just hanging out, playing cards or dominoes (popular with the Latinos) or sitting quietly. Unlike social life in pubs, restaurants and parties, the American naval variety lacked the essential ingredient that fuels the ascent from tentative initial exchanges to vehemently expressed opinions, to outpouring of affection, muddled thinking and eventual fisticuffs: alcohol! We've all been to parties and dinners where one or two people are not drinking but a party where *everyone* is off the sauce? Shit, you might as well convert to radical Islam and get intoxicated— git the high—on that.

Just as I'd assumed there would be Ping-Pong tables and badminton courts on board so I'd also hoped that there would be bars. Or at least *a* bar. That's where I pictured myself hanging out after playing Ping-Pong, getting stories from tongue-loosened sailors like an old-fashioned Fleet Street hack, running up a tab and claiming it all on expenses back at the beach. A single day on board was enough to disabuse me of this fantasy; the idea of allowing booze on the boat seemed insane—though I gathered that British and Australian ships did permit a certain amount of drinking.

It wasn't just that there was no booze—there were none of the trappings or decorations of alcohol, none of the things that make you want to linger in bars and pubs. This was not life as we know it or want it, where drinks at six or seven p.m. signal the transition from the working day to leisure time, to being free to do whatever you want (get fucked up!).

So there we were in an environment unconducive to carousing, watched always by armed security guys who kept an eye on things, making sure nothing got out of hand either competitively (dominoes is a potentially explosive pastime), argumentatively or romantically (the 'Rules to Live By' were prominently displayed).

The nearest thing to a bar was the Lone Star Café, a Starbucks concession serving decent coffee. It looked OK but whenever Paul proposed we go by it was closed or the opposite of closed in that the line was too long, or it was too late in the day for me to drink coffee without frying my brain. If, on the basis of my two-week residency, I ever get asked to design a carrier I'll create more places like this, places that look properly like bars, cosy red-signed environments with lots of neon so you can feel like you're in an episode of *Cheers* and enjoy a mirage of life back home.

Everyone talked of missing their families. If these guys were to be believed their families were the only things they missed about life back on the beach. No one said they missed restaurants or bars, meeting up with friends or going out to parties and nightclubs. But even though people on the boat had kids when they were young and got married even younger, plenty of people on board must have been childless and single, must have missed hanging out with their friends, going out and getting drunk, picking up girls—or boys—and having casual sex. And what about other things: windows with views, trees, weekends, going for a drive, sitting in a park reading a book, access to online porn, buying groceries from a stall at the market, trying on clothes in shops, walking home at night as it's about to rain and getting to your door just as it starts pouring? No one mentioned this stuff—because they could not bear to? Because the torment of missing these things was so great that they could never be spoken of?

On the way back from one of my fruitless expeditions to the Lone Star Café with Paul and the snapper I bumped into the woman from the hangar deck with the luminous eyes and the ex-Marine husband. It was not the first time this had happened.

The story that I'd been told about two brothers serving on the same carrier for seven months without ever running into each other might have been a nautical urban legend. The carrier wasn't *that* big and, in the course of a day, one ran into a lot of people—or I did, at least. My days, admittedly, were rather different from most people's in that they involved tooling round the ship with Paul, meeting and greeting as though I were actually being groomed for some nonexistent mayoral office: *Hi, how are you? What are the things about the ship that really concern you? I understand. These are exactly the things that concern me. I hope I can count on your vote*. It was not just that I ran into a lot of people; I kept running into a lot of the *same* people. Not because I was confined to the business-class or officers-only section of the boat but because that's the way it happened—that's the way *life* happens.

In particular I *kept* bumping into the woman from the hangar bay. Maybe I ran into other people from her work detail or section as well, but I was only conscious of bumping into her. Her eyes always seemed to have a special I'm-happy-to-see-you glow about them, which may have been no more than a reflection of the extra wattage that seeing her always brought into my own eyes. I'm not deluded—there was no reason on earth why, with her ex-Marine husband and kid at home, her eyes should have lit up at the sight of this aged civilian (old enough to be her father, with probably five or ten years to spare). No, no reason at all. She was one of those people who have that extra glow but *the fact* is that I kept running into her and these meetings constituted one of my daily or bi-daily highlights.

27

Sunday night. I was deeply asleep, my ears were stuffed, as usual, with wax earplugs, but the announcement on the Main Circuit was clear, loud, unignorable.

'*Man overboard, man overboard.*'

The next bit was clear to everyone on the boat except me: something about muster stations. Immediately there was a tramping and rumble of feet and then, again:

'*Man overboard, man overboard. Time: plus one.*'

The human voice—not prerecorded or automated—was calm and authoritative, a perfect combination of urgency and zero panic. Not knowing what else to do—it was probably a drill in any case—I just lay there. Another minute passed.

'*Time: plus two.*'

Then Paul knocked on my door.

'Is this a drill?' I asked, hiding, naked, behind the door.

'No, this is the real thing. But best just to stay in your stateroom.'

'*Time: plus three.*'

I went back to my rack, that lovely life raft, while everyone else hurried to wherever they were meant to be. There was nothing to do except think of being the person alone in the dark ocean. Better, in a way, to die with others as the *Titanic* went down, or on a merchant ship after it had been torpedoed by the wolf pack.

'*Time: plus four.*'

I lay on my rack, hearing more footsteps on the stairs, listening to time pass. I remembered Cowper's 'Castaway'—'Of friends, of hope, of all bereft, / His floating home for ever left'—

and Golding's *Pincher Martin:* 'He didn't even have time to kick off his sea boots.'

Rescue boats, presumably, were being lowered and launched, swimmers readied.

'*Time: plus five.*' And then: '*The following individuals report to the quarterdeck with your ID card. From Combat Systems: ET3 Denny; from Supply: ET2 Luskin, AD3 Smith; from Air: ADAN Fletcher; from Ops: OSSN Lucas ...* ' I lost track of the names, perhaps ten or a dozen of them, the unaccounted for, the missing.

'*Time: plus six.*'

The list was repeated with a few names added and a few removed until, after this brief interlude of expansion and contraction, it began inexorably to shrink—six names, then five—as fate converged on fewer and fewer people:

'*The following individuals report to the quarterdeck with your ID card. From Supply: ET2 Luskin, AD3 Smith; from Ops: OSSN Lucas ...* ' It was like listening to the ball rattling round a roulette wheel, waiting to hear where—on whom—it would land.

Time continued to pass, to mount with no increase or diminution of either urgency or desperation:

'*Time: plus eight.*'

Nothing to do but lie on my rack, comfortable—dry and warm—in the knowledge that I was not drowning, that I was accounted for, that my number was not up, that my time had not come.

Then, sounding distinctly irritated (but immediately recognizable as the man who each day proclaimed that it was another great day to be at sea): 'From the bridge of the USS *George Bush,* this is the Captain. Hey, anyone throwing anything over the side of this ship needs to stop *right* now.'

By '*Time: plus eleven*' the list of the missing had shrunk to just two: '*The following individuals report to the quarterdeck with your ID card. From Supply: ET2 Luskin, AD3 Smith.*'

Lying in my rack. Alive.

'Time: plus twelve.'

'Will the following report to the quarterdeck with your ID card. From Supply: AD3 Smith.'

So that was it. If there was a man overboard it was AD3 Smith for whom time was not increasing but counting down, running out. One person out of five thousand.

At *'Time: plus eighteen'* the Captain came on the Main Circuit again:

'A float coat has been picked up. We have a complete and full muster of all hands on board. We'll look into the float coat issue and will secure from the mustering portion of the man overboard.'

So Smith had turned up. Everyone was safe, present and—the phrase had never seemed so caring—*accounted for*. I lay on my rack. The sound of accounted-for footsteps resumed outside, in the corridors of the living, up and down the stairs of the breathing. There were no more announcements. Time resumed its usual unaccounted-for passing.

28

At breakfast next morning, with my knack for idiotic pleasantry, anchored in zero knowledge, I remarked that accounting for every one of the five thousand crew in eighteen minutes was extremely fast. In fact it had been a slow muster and should have been done in fifteen minutes. Oh.

One of the reasons it should have been done more quickly is that these man-overboard alerts were not as uncommon as might be supposed. On one ship a dissatisfied pair from maintenance had thrown float coats or ChemLights overboard on three successive nights as a form of protest. On another there had been a suicide: someone wrapped himself in chains from the flight deck and jumped into the ocean. (So much *more* of a death, somehow, than Virginia Woolf stepping into the Ouse with a pocket full of stones.)

'Like the Jonah in *Master and Commander*,' I ventured. (For some reason I was desperate to have my say this morning.) The body was never found but a note had been left. Another would-be suicide had a change of heart. As soon as he hit the water, he went into the survival drill that he'd learned in boot camp (taking off his boots and trousers, tying the legs and inflating them over his head), survived three hours in the water and found himself in deep shit when he was eventually picked up after a night—to say the least—of profoundly mixed emotions. (Which wise-ass philosopher said he was in favour of suicide on the principled grounds of people's right to make mistakes?)

Emboldened by the coffee, by the relative success of my *Master and Commander* remark (it had been neither applauded nor ridiculed) and by the generally relaxed vibe, I ventured another ex cathedra observation: namely that it is quite hard to fall overboard by accident. And this time I got it right! It *is*. Unless you're blown overboard by jet blast. That can happen: a blast of scalding hot air with the force to blow you off your feet and over the side, a fifty-foot drop and then an unspecified amount of time in shark-and-jellyfish-infested seas: for the accident-prone adrenaline junkie that must score pretty high.

29

The man overboard scare was representative of life on ship in several ways.

An exceptional event was dealt with by the meticulous application of endlessly rehearsed routine. So frequent are the rehearsals—and so seriously are they taken—that the distinction between practice and 'the real thing' (as Paul called it) is all but irrelevant. (Even to ask the question, as I did, is a sign of being an outsider: a waste of time, which, the announcements made clear, was absolutely of the essence.)

Also: there is never a dull moment. But this translates into: there is never a moment's peace, no guarantee of a good night's sleep. There is never a dull moment, and yet life is an endless succession of dull moments (the idea is to make even the most unexpected emergency a matter of routine), especially for those sweeping the decks, or cleaning, wiping, washing, shining. Day after day, for seven months.

This was confirmed when I accompanied two of the security guys, Chris and Myrl, on their rounds. They looked pretty mean, biologically disposed and militarily programmed to cut no slack, to listen indifferently to lame-ass excuses before getting down to the serious business of meting out punishment. (Chris in particular—I say 'Chris' but, in truth, I am struggling now to remember who was who—had the look of a sausage that had been fried without being pricked, with the attendant risk of bursting.) That's how they seemed at first but in the course of our time together I came to see that their facial expressions were part of the uniform, something they put on each day prior to going to work.

We started off where I'd first seen them, in the mess hall, empty now because it was being cleaned. The tables and chairs constituted a single hinged unit with seats angled up over the tables—to facilitate cleaning—like the wings of jets on the flight deck. From there we went on a tour of the nooks and crannies where people stashed alcohol, and the linen cupboards where they had been caught making out.

'We know all the sneak spots,' Myrl said. 'Sometimes we find two couples in these remote places.'

'*Two* couples? Wow! There are swingers on the boat?'

'I mean two people, excuse me. *A* couple.' It seemed more likely that we would come across not double couples but half couples: solitary crew members who were not even looking for a spot to jerk off but who just wanted a place where they could be on their own. Chris and Myrl—who spent more time together than a married couple—understood this need.

'The only time you get any privacy is in the head or in the rack,' said Chris. We came across a fire extinguisher whose tamper-proof thing had been tampered with. We checked out a refuelling sponson which, as Myrl said, was 'another popular sneak spot.' That said it all. Even the places where you hoped to get some time with your secret sweetheart or on your own were 'popular'.

We plodded around. There was nothing much going on, nothing out of place, but this was to be expected. It was only when the ship pulled into port that Chris and Myrl's jobs got interesting—in two quite contrary ways. The boat had to be guarded because this was when it was most at risk from ter-rorist attack. And you had all the sailors coming back drunk. They were encouraged to have just one drink an hour (which, in writerly circles, sounds like taking the pledge) and the Navy encouraged them to come back on the ship rather than spend the night ashore—with all the attendant possibilities of having much more fun and getting into lots more trouble. So if they could follow proper procedures, if they were sober enough to ask permission to come aboard, and not meander too much, that was fine.

Chris and Myrl were young guys—twenty-seven and twenty-three respectively—who had wanted to be cops; but both said several times that they were here not to bust their shipmates but to help them out.

'The difference between any of us and being behind bars,' said Chris (who, I repeat, might have been Myrl), 'is one bad day.'

Our patrol had been uneventful in the extreme. As so often with Navy life boredom seemed the worst enemy but even worse than boredom—so much worse that it was unthinkable—was the idea that it might be pointless. All the drills, the redundancy and patrols and the checking—you have to put out of people's minds the idea that *anything* might be a waste of time, that any of it could be skipped. This it turns out is surprisingly easy, for a carrier—or any military institution—exists in a state of constant potential threat (of accidents or attack) and it's only by making the responses routine that these threats can be dealt with calmly when they are realized. So a successful deployment in which no lives are lost and no one is seriously injured resembles nothing else so much as an endless series of dress rehearsals for a performance (a real fire, say) that is *less* dramatic than any of the simulations leading up to it. Day in day out, people toil away, making the rounds on the boat that is going round and round in a bit of sea, on a planet that is also doing its rounds. W. H. Auden said that poetry makes nothing happen, and much of what happens on a carrier is dedicated to turning the boat into a poem (another reason for the renaming suggested earlier?), to making sure that nothing happens. So round and round we go (just as I'd gone round and round in the helo a few days earlier) with Chris and Myrl doing their bit, scouting out sneak spots and linen-cupboard liaisons, not expecting to find anything and glad, in a disappointed sort of way, when they don't. Along the corridors, around the catwalks and up and down the stairs they go, chipping away at the days of this vast and orbital deployment, getting one day nearer to going home to see the year-old daughter who is keeping in step, doing her bit (though in one direction only), growing one day older.

30

We were a few minutes late for the FOD (foreign object debris) walk. By the time we got up on the flight deck there was a line of helmeted and vizored people, three or four deep, stretched across the bow of the boat, starting to walk towards us. (Ah, so *this* was the flight-deck promenade that we had observed from the helo a couple of days previously!) It was like Pellizza da Volpedo's painting *The Fourth Estate,* re-enacted in some brightly coloured sci-fi future. Our cranials meant that it was silent as a painting too. A rainbow coalition of float coats, shirts and helmets—all framed by the horizon of sea and sky—it was a thoroughly impressive display of human-technological might but, since everyone was walking slowly, heads bowed, it was reminiscent, also, of something seen from time to time on TV news: a line of police officers combing the countryside in a similarly orderly line, looking for clues after a school kid has gone missing, oblivious to the bucolic surroundings, conscious only of what they are looking for.

And so it was here. They inched forward. No one looked up, everyone was concentrating on finding the bit of metal or trash that had somehow ended up on deck and which could find its way into a jet's air intakes. The planes were unbelievably powerful but this power co-existed with a heightened vulnerability and susceptibility to sudden and catastrophic failure. 'It takes about 80,000 rivets, 30,000 washers, 10,000 screws and bolts to help make an aircraft fly,' read posters scattered round the boat, 'and only one nut to destroy it.'

The line of silent people advanced towards us, a slow-moving force of anti-nature. We stood our ground and then turned and joined the hunt. A couple of guys held leather pouches. When people found something—a piece of metal, small bits of stone, stuff too small even to have a name—they held it up and dropped it in a pouch. I was reminded of the Burning Man festival in the Black Rock Desert with its scrupulous adherence to the policy of Leave No Trace and a similar obsession with MOOP (Matter Out Of Place).

It was a lovely day—it was a lovely day every day—but there was no time, at the end of the FOD walk, to just hang out, stroll around, enjoy the view. People dispersed quickly, went back to their sunless submarine life below deck.

On the way back to my room I paused to listen to the Captain's daily announcement. 'It's a bee-oo-tiful day to be at sea,' he said. 'A *striking* day. I think we ought to send our paychecks back to the Navy for the privilege of being at sea today.'

31

It had not escaped my attention that everybody on the boat had the teeth of Hollywood stars: white, straight, gleaming, uniformly perfect. Paul and I went down to the surgery to see how this orthodontic excellence and anonymity was produced and maintained. The walls of the reception were crammed with vari-coloured folders full of the crew's dental histories. Just as I was thinking that it *looked* like a dentist's in England—old-fashioned and ordinary—I saw something extraordinary: someone *older* than me, disappearing down a corridor. At last! Bryan Foster, the young guy showing me round, confirmed this sighting: there was indeed a sixty-year-old dentist on board. Sixty, by American standards, is not old, but in a context where the average age is about twenty-two he looked *ancient,* like an elder from a village in Afghanistan or a prophet left behind from some previous era of human development before the youth inherited the earth and took over the ship.

As for Bryan—nice, normal-aged Bryan—he'd been in Afghanistan for eight months, spending some of that time in Helmand with British forces, dealing with combat casualties.

'Facial injuries, that kind of thing?' I said, assuming that combat demanded that his area of expertise perhaps extended to the zone around the mouth and teeth.

'No, everything, sir. Tourniquets, amputations, disembowelments, IED blasts—everything you can think of. A lot of the enlisted sailors you'll see down here are trained in dental *and* combat casualty care. We're expected to be able to do everything.'

I had discovered, over the course of the previous three or four years, how deeply I admired many of the soldiers that I had read about in books or seen in documentaries about Iraq or Afghanistan. But always, just as impressive as the fighting soldiers were the medics: the military doctors whose job was to patch together their mutilated comrades, luckless civilians caught up in fighting and, on occasion, their enemies. Bryan had done all of that and still managed to guide me round his current place of work as though nothing gave him more pride and satisfaction than the outstanding quality of orthodontics on offer. People sometimes talk of feeling 'humbled', but that's not how I felt on the boat; it was more like an awareness of frequently being in the presence of superior individuals whose capacities and experience were quite unlike those I came across—I knew plenty of writers and artists—back at the beach.

As Bryan showed me the various treatment rooms where patients were having teeth painlessly drilled and cleaned, their chewing and smiling potential enhanced, I was conscious of something else that often happened in the course of my assignment: I was not concentrating on what I was seeing and hearing. Instead of diligently making notes and asking questions about the way the surgery was run I was mentally rehearsing a pitch whereby maybe, as part of my research, if a slot was available, it would be useful, *as part of my research,* to get my crooked English teeth checked out, cleaned and polished. When I did finally raise the possibility Bryan considered it an excellent idea, was only too happy to demonstrate the excellence of the service provided. He looked through the schedule of appointments and asked if I could come back at eight. I looked at the clock. It was just after six. Consider this for a moment: I was being offered an appointment *two hours from now*. No, that is not a mistake. He did not mean two months, two weeks or two days—he meant two *hours*. I booked in, smiling my crooked, yellowy, freeloading English smile.

'Oh there's one more thing,' I said to Bryan. 'That old guy

we saw? I hoped I'd get a chance to speak with him.' I didn't really have anything to ask him except the gloating questions 'What's it like to be so old?' or 'Hey, old-timer, how's it feel to be the oldest guy on the boat?' Bryan looked around but he was nowhere to be seen. And he wasn't there when I returned to the surgery later that evening. He was never anywhere to be seen. And so he took on the quality of an apparition or ghost, a figment of my imagination, a spirit I'd conjured up to make myself feel younger.

A sword-and-sorcery/martial-arts epic was on TV when I went back to the surgery. The volume was turned way up—not to cover up the dreadful sound of drilling and screams but because this was a carrier where any TV worthy of the name was cranked up like the PA at Glastonbury. I filled out a load of forms, joked that I hoped I wasn't signing anything that meant I was liable for the full cost of labour and materials (ha ha!), was shown into a room and introduced to HM1 Wang, who tipped me back in the chair and went to work. It was the same kind of thing I'd had done in London—scraping and picking with prodders, deep-whiz polishing, flossing and, for dessert, a gobful of some kind of high-intensity fluoride trifle—but it felt more treat than treatment, or at least like a treatment in the spa sense of the word. You know that feeling when you're having a massage or some utterly superfluous pamper-therapy and you feel time floating away? When you think you could lie there for the rest of eternity? That's pretty much how I felt here, as if some impacted wisdom chakras were being painlessly unblocked. Certainly it's the only time I have ever been to a dentist's and wished I could have been there longer, had more done. What a shame it was just a clean, that there wasn't some root canal work to be undertaken or an Amisian crown and bridge to be installed, a potentially agonizing experience (both physically and financially) that would have been rendered entirely painless by both the skill of the dentist and the knowledge that I was getting it entirely for free.

The hour passed horribly quickly. The seat went back to upright mode. I looked in the mirror at my gleaming, whiter-than-they-had-ever-been (but still crooked), happy, almost-American teeth. Was this another reason why they were always smiling on the carrier—to show off their teeth? Back in the reception it really was, as they say, smiles all round. I was even presented with a full set of dental records as a souvenir.

It was nine thirty. I returned to my room and, for the first time in forty years, went to bed without cleaning my teeth.

32

The most crowded place on this crowded ship was the smoke pit: a little area towards the stern of the boat, on the starboard side, maybe five yards by five, with room for about twenty people to stand and smoke. (This is hearsay; it sounded so disgusting I didn't set foot on it myself.) The queue to get out there was always immense, like the lines of junkies waiting to score crack or heroin in *The Wire*. There is a long-running connection between the Navy and smoking (the Player's cigarettes my mum used to smoke actually had a sailor on the packet) but it seemed odd that the Navy didn't simplify matters and declare the ship smoke-free. People would be cranky for a bit but after a while the craving for nicotine would pass and they would be relieved of this compulsion to waste so much of the little free time they had queuing up to smoke. The counter-argument is that smoking is a pleasure, one of few available during a sexless and boozeless deployment. Well, *exactly:* if you can go without booze and sex then why not go without smoking too? Especially since cigarettes are not a source of pleasure. A cigarette serves mainly to alleviate the craving for a cigarette, removes the pain of wanting a cigarette. Take away the cigarette and you take away the craving too. But, hey, what do I know? I've never had one.

The incredible thing was that these smokers could have been enjoying the smokeless air of the fantail instead. This idyllic spot was always so empty that I'd assumed people were not allowed out there—but they were, apparently, except when planes were landing, when there was a chance of a jet smashing into the back of the boat and causing a mass of casualties. Even tonight, less than a minute's walk from the smoke pit, there were just the guys on watch, looking out over a barely swaying sea. An oil well was perched on the horizon, glowing redly like a miniature sun, a fraction of the size of the eye-frying whopper we're used to. It was like a dream of the astrophysical future when the sun had used itself up, run out of gas, was just an ember of its former self. It cast a dim reddish glow, hardly enough to illuminate the dark clouds of oil pollution that loured over it. Its days were numbered whereas the moon was in the ascendant: sharp as a disc and creating a foil glitter of our wake. In its low-key, not-with-a-bang-barely-even-a-whimper way, it was one of the most apocalyptic sights I had ever seen.

Planes came in to land. Each, at first, was an orange blob of light, then a horizontal line of traffic lights—green, amber, red—and finally a solid roar of light screaming directly overhead.[*]

As the days passed, I sought out more and more opportunities to hang out on the fantail, to turn my deployment into a kind of pleasure cruise with military accessories thrown in. On the flimsiest pretext I would ask to be escorted there so that I could sit on a capstan and gaze at the sea and sky: the turquoise foam bath of the carrier's wake, sometimes a tanker perched idly on the horizon, the constantly circling helos. I never quite had the nerve to don my headphones and listen to the nautical playlist I'd prepared prior to boarding (and which I'd never listened to), though I probably could have got away with it under the pretext of putting Bose's patented noise-cancelling system through its paces.

The monotony of life at sea is not confined to the jobs people do. Seeing the sun rise and set every day in the unchanging sky over the unchanging—and constantly changing—ocean

---

[*] I had permission to be there while the planes were landing.

is inherently meditative, and it was easy to fall into a cognitive trance out there on the fantail. (Actually, for many members of the crew, busy toiling away below decks, part of that sentence needs to be rewritten as follows: '*Not* seeing the sun rise and set every day in the unseen sky over the unseen ocean . . . ' The sea, for many—probably most—of the sailors working in its midst was conspicuous by its absolute absence from their lives, except as the thing that obliged them to remain within the confines of the boat.) In my case this fantail trance took the form of a kind of mental seasickness whereby the clarity and fixity of the carrier's unquestioned purpose gave rise to feelings—and questions—of purposelessness. Did the presence of these carrier-launched planes in the skies over Iraq accomplish anything at this moment in history (especially if one considered the actual and opportunity costs of doing so)? Wasn't it in some ways an unbelievably expensive and noisy provocation? Weren't the planes flying missions primarily because the boat was here and because that's what planes do? This in turn raised other doubts about the constant guarding against risk and threat. The carrier would not have been at risk if it had not been here.

So there I was: a tourist with a notebook, a marine anthropologist whose data was so thoroughly and distortingly mixed up with the means of obtaining it that it probably had no value as data, only as a memoir or a collection of camera-less holiday snaps. *Here's one of me and Newell on the flight deck. Oh, here's one of me on the fantail with a guy whose name I can't quite remember . . .*

But lest we forget—lest I forgot—I was not without rank, purpose and station. G. Dyer (FRSL) was writer-in-residence and by residing here (on the fantail, whenever possible) and scrawling in his school exercise books he was *doing his duty,* serving his country (or, at the very least, fulfilling the terms of his contract).

And it was not all plain sailing out there on the fantail, underneath the scorching sun. Iranian boats would come close—whatever 'close' means in naval terms—as a test and provocation. The pot, in this instance, seemed to be calling the kettle black. We were in international waters, but at some points (I had heard) we were only twenty-eight miles off the coast of Iran. We were a big-ass warship capable of raining death and destruction on people's heads twenty-four hours a day; we spent our time strutting round the Gulf like we owned the place; and our planes (to put the matter mildly) made a helluva racket. I'd have loved nothing more than to have seen Ahmadinejad step into a specially convened boxing ring on the flight deck and get his bearded ass kicked by one of the crew (a woman ideally) but, in the larger scheme of things, it seemed that our presence might be construed as provocative or, at the very least, intrusive. How would we have felt if the Eye-ranians had a carrier twenty-eight miles off the coast of Maine or Cornwall? Would we have tolerated that kind of stunt even for a millisecond?

33

I got used to showering in the noisy, smelly bathrooms—with my flip-flops on in case of verrucas—but it was an experience devoid of pleasure. I never lingered, always tried to get out before anyone else came in. When it came to crapping I always picked a corner stall, figuring that a person on one side rather than both offered a 50 per cent increase in privacy. It was awful, sitting there, to see a pair of heavy black boots beneath the door of the opposite stall or the panel separating me from the stall next door, knowing someone else was engaged in a facing or parallel dump. The contrast that I'd been so conscious of in the gym, between my scrawny limbs and those of the grunting pumpers, also made itself felt here in the so-called head. Living on a subsistence diet, I alternated between manageable diarrhoea and stringy little turds. The sailors who were tucking daily into their burgers and hot dogs, meanwhile, were sitting there solidly—feet planted on the ground, straining away like weightlifters—and depositing swollen bicep turds that put the vacuum system through its paces. The gym ethos permeated the ship: the food gave the digestive capacities of the body a daily workout; at times, faced with the sheer amount of grease and fat confronting it, the digestive system must have been tempted to call it a day, but then the military training kicked in and the body had to suck it up, had to start breaking this stuff down, translating it into energy and power which was then put to work in the gyms and exercise classes until eventually the unusable residue—of which there was a vast amount—was bench-pressed into shape and passed on to the vacuum system which, in turn, was in the grips of a constant, system-threatening workout that frequently left it prostrate and constipated, in a state of total collapse.

I lost track of the number of times my local toilets were out of action. Often enough to make me approach them with a feeling of mounting anxiety which turned either to dread (what am I gonna do now?) when confronted with a notice on the locked door or relief (they're working!) when the door opened and the promise of a fully functioning toilet made itself pongily apparent.

The state of the toilets was the single biggest source of grievance while I was on the boat, and it continued to be a contentious issue after I'd returned to the exquisite privacy of my owner-occupier lavatory at home. The mother of one of the sailors wrote a blog about the state of the toilets and how they were adversely affecting the mental and physical well-being of the crew (faced with a lack of toilet opportunities, they were drinking less and therefore becoming dehydrated). This blog found its way onto various media outlets, prompting the Captain to send a fifteen-hundred-word response on Facebook to family and friends of the crew. It's a remarkable document, notable for statistical precision, the vigour with which speed of repair is presented and defended, and the thoroughness with which causes of blockage are itemized:

> Inappropriate items that have been flushed down the commode and caused clogs during deployment include feminine hygiene products and their applicators, mop heads, T-shirts, underwear, towels, socks, hard-boiled eggs, and eating utensils.
> There have been ZERO (0) clogs caused by toilet paper and human waste.

As for claims of 'increased health issues, such as dehydration, and increased urinary tract infections', the Captain simultaneously rebuts the claim and offers an alternative explanation for why the last-mentioned might have arisen: 'There have been 60 total cases of urinary tract infection during deployment with two major spikes occurring immediately following port visits.'

34

I went to see Fish the Bish again—at his suggestion. As I sat down I noticed a quotation from John Wesley taped to the wall over his desk: a faultless creed, gently in keeping with the exhortations to excellence seen elsewhere on the boat:

> Do all the good you can
> By all the means you can
> In all the ways you can
> In all the places you can
> At all the times you can
> To all the people you can
> As long as ever you can.

Even though we were speaking at close range—three feet max—his eyes were always fixed on the middle distance and, as befits a man of faith, his gaze would often turn upward. This was all the more striking since there was no middle distance: we were in his small, low-ceilinged office so the maximum depth of focus required was maybe a couple of yards. But that is what faith does: it enables you to see the bigger picture and expand your horizons (though when there are no horizons in view this could be counted as a delusion). It also suggests that the other person—in this case, me—is not an individual but a congregation, that the chair Fish was sitting on was some kind of pulpit. I don't mean to be uncharitable. Maybe if I'd gone to him with a specific problem, if I'd been in need of pastoral care or help, he'd have looked me in the eye and put a theologically comforting arm around my shoulder. But in this context he was there not to console or chat but to hold forth. I was especially conscious of this when he explained that chaplains in the British Navy assume the rank of the person they are with. This seemed more American than British and yet I had the sense, throughout our audience, of being outranked.

When I asked him about the people who came to see him he told me about the ones who didn't. It was hard to persuade officers to come because of their 'zero-defect mentality'. The chiefs—sailors who started out as enlisted men and had worked their way up to E-7 or E-9—were reluctant to come, too, as they were grounded in 'an older, tougher style of man-management'. Which left, I suppose, almost everyone else. And often it wasn't that they had specific—let alone religious—problems.

'Something about being at sea, especially standing a long watch, encourages us to think of big questions,' he said. Not for the first time I found that someone I was speaking to was making a point that I had intuited myself. It was good to have my fantail belief confirmed by . . . well, by a higher authority, I guess.

Perhaps the key part of the Bish's operation was that what was said to him had the status of a Confession, freeing people to speak in confidence in an environment in which it was hard to keep anything private. If at the end of their sessions people talking to the Bish decided they needed to see the ship's psychiatrist then he went too. 'But I don't lead and I don't follow—I walk alongside.' (How he managed this in the crowded and narrow corridors of the boat was not something I felt I could raise: I liked the idea and took the point.)

I'd warmed to the Bish as our conversation proceeded—and that, it seemed, was not uncommon. According to the Bish many of the people who sought him out ended up by saying, ' "Chaps, I don't know what it is, but it's good to have you around." But if they ask for better weather I have to tell them I'm in sales, not production.'

———

'So, will you walk with me to the psychiatrist?' I said to the Bish as I got up to leave. I wasn't cracking up and I wasn't cracking wise either: I actually had an appointment but was unsure how to get there. The fact that it was a happy ship did not mean that everyone aboard was happy; I wanted to see another strand in the pastoral/disciplinary safety net that kept the ship functioning smoothly.

The psychiatrist was one of the most civilian-seeming people on the boat, a young guy whose hair looked fashionably rather than militarily short. He was Brandon Heck, a lieutenant, more widely known as 'the Psych'. Unlike the Bish, who'd sung like a canary, the Psych kept his cards so close to his chest they were behind his back. More in the habit of asking questions than answering them, he had a way of responding that fulfilled the minimum conditions of a reply without any elaboration or excess. He did this without recourse to the technical language of psychiatry, so the effect was to minimize any disturbances or problems people had. This, for all I knew, was part of the treatment he offered, a preemptive way of normalizing the abnormal. I wasn't with him long.

Since for many people joining the Navy was 'an alternative to going to college', the main problem, he said, was simply one of 'adjusting to living away from home for the first time, especially in a place where sitting outside listening to birds is just not an option'—not with the roar of birds launching and recovering it wasn't. People were 'still in high school mindset—banding together in certain divisive ways.' With problems de-emphasized in this way the solution was correspondingly reduced from a cure to finding a way, 'stressful as this environment is, to something they can get comfortable with.'

In keeping with this I came away from my brief session with the Psych believing that I hadn't needed to see him at all.

Or would have done were it not for one aspect of the current deployment that, he said, caused 'particular challenges'. This was the practice of individual augmentation whereby individual crew members sent to Afghanistan in Marine or Army units had encountered and experienced things without any of the group preparation and support that is such a crucial part of life in the USMC and or the infantry. Parachuted in, as it were, and airlifted out afterwards, they were left to process what had happened individually, back in the company of an entirely different set of people from whom they had earlier been removed.

As it happened I'd recently read *What It Is Like to Go to War* in which Karl Marlantes writes about something similar happening *within* the Army and the Marines. In the Second World War people came home slowly, gradually, by boat, as part of a unit. In Vietnam, and in Iraq and Afghanistan, the swift return and dispersal of the group was accelerated and increased, something that may well have played a part in the drastic increase in PTSD. To counter this, Marlantes believes, there is a need for a similarly ritualized reversal of the process by which young men were transformed into fighting machines in order to reassimilate them to civilian life once more. I mentioned this to the Psych. In fact, listening to the tape again, I realized that I spent longer telling the Psych about Marlantes's diagnosis and proposed cure than he had telling me about the problem of individual augmentation in the first place. At the end of my exhaustive summary, you can just about hear the Psych, barely audible above the usual background din, nodding over steepled fingers, saying, 'Uh-huh.'

That night I couldn't sleep. I kept thinking back to the man-overboard scare, of a lone sailor, drifting towards death in the ocean's heaving blackness.

I had an iPod crammed full of music but had ended up,

whenever I had time, always listening to the same thing: Sviato-slav Richter playing Bach's *Forty-Eight Preludes and Fugues*. It's not difficult to work out why I'd narrowed down my choice of music to this one thing that, like the sea, is forever changing into some other thing. From the first notes of the opening prelude you are not just listening to music; you have entered a differ-ent realm, a realm of absolute perfection—of constantly altering perfection—in which nothing sucks or has to be sucked up. (The same, obviously, cannot be said of Beethoven who was drawn, relentlessly, to the enormous suck of the world and the self.) On this night, though, I couldn't sleep and I couldn't lose myself in the music intended as a substitute for sleep. I kept thinking of a castaway lost in the vastness of the sea until this image turned into an identical and opposite scenario. A ship goes down with all hands—except one. The lone individual floating in the sea is actually the sole survivor, as in the line from the Book of Job quoted by Melville in the epilogue to *Moby-Dick*: 'And I only am escaped alone to tell thee.'

35

It was actually the snapper who was escaping, whose deployment was coming to an end. One of the last pictures he took before heading back to the beach was the one he'd had in mind right from the start, from our first morning on the boat: the infinite mirror of corridors, at night, lit by the red glow of safety lights, when there was little foot traffic and a long exposure allowed the walkways to reflect on their own immensity. I'd been struck by this hall-of-mirrors thing myself, had jotted down variants of that phrase—'infinite-mirror effect', 'tunnel of mirrors'—in my exercise book. It was a good thing to have noticed. Then, after I got back to the beach myself, I read Tom Wolfe's 1975 essay 'The Truest Sport: Jousting with Sam and Charlie', about pilots flying missions from a carrier during the Vietnam War. Wolfe had been through the walkways too, had noticed the way that 'as you look on and through these hatchways, one after the other, it's like a hall of mirrors.'

I read it with a steady *oh shit* sensation of self-confidence draining away. And the hatchways were only part of my worries. I'd ended up feeling less conspicuous on the boat, not Didion-ly invisible but more at ease and confident around the people I ran into every day. I cracked more jokes, expressed my personality a bit more. The downside was that I'd ended up feeling less and less confident about the work I was supposed to be doing. For the previous year or so I had been more admiring of the books of reportage coming out of Afghanistan and Iraq—by David Finkel, Dexter Filkins, Evan Wright and others—than almost any of the novels I'd been reading in the same period. What skill it took to notice and to record stuff, often in the midst of danger that was real and immediate. Whereas I had trouble recording even the simplest things such as someone's name and rank. The longer I spent on the carrier the more convinced I became that, of all the kinds of writer I was not, 'reporter' was top of the list.

As a reporter Wolfe also had the advantage that his pilots were flying real combat missions and ended up getting shot down and ejecting over the sea, but there was no getting away from the simple, noncircumstantial truth: 'The Truest Sport' was a brilliant piece of reporting and writing, impossible to improve on except insofar as ... I got myself into a right old state; the way that I kept circling back to that phrase 'except insofar as' was proof of that. I mean, what kind of phrase was that? What kind of writer would use that, even once, except one who was caught like a rabbit in the headlights of another writer's brilliance. 'Like a rabbit in the headlights ... ' I was in the infinite feedback loop, a mirror-hall of self-doubt, intensified by the way Wolfe improved on his unimprovable essay with *The Right Stuff*.

Taking off and landing from a carrier had gotten safer since the time of Wolfe's essay—it had already gotten safer *by* the time Wolfe was writing his piece—but in essentials the carrier experience hadn't changed significantly since Vietnam, or since the Second World War. It's all about noisy planes taking off and landing on a flat platform in the middle of the ocean—Wolfe likens it not to a postage stamp but to 'a heaving, greasy skillet'—and large numbers of people living together in cramped conditions, eating greasy-skillet food. Photographs of life on board a carrier in the build-up to the Battle of Midway are remarkably like ones you could take today, like the ones the snapper had been snapping. Allow for small adjustments in clothing and technology and the pictures were practically identical.

Much is made of the swagger and confidence of pilots, especially Navy pilots, the ones who land on carriers the size of postage stamps or skillets. But confidence is essential to writing too. You can't do it without talent but you can't do it without confidence either—and Wolfe had taken a shark-sized bite out of mine. Once your confidence goes other things start to go with it. You fall into depression. You begin to dread the page, the words, the futility of putting the latter on the former. I was like a pilot in the process of losing it: the veteran of thousands of arrested landings and catapulted lunches—I mean *launches*—who just can't do it anymore. Who gets the shakes at the mere thought of being hurled off the deck and into the black dog of night. Constantly on the brink of seeing the Bish or the Psych and telling them that he can't do it anymore, that a zero-defect mentality has given way to a zero-ability mentality, to zero ability. Lying awake at night knowing that the thing he is—a pilot, a Navy pilot—is really the thing he *was,* that it's only a matter of time before others find out too. So by the time he gets suited up and ready to go he's already exhausted and used up. Climbs into the cockpit, connects all the tubes and harnessing, goes through the checks and is shocked to discover, all over again, what he's been discovering for a while now: that there's no place on earth he'd rather not be. Still able to process all the information and data coming his way from the flight deck and the instrument panels but none of it sufficient to drown out the words that are sounding through his head: Abort, Abort, Abort and Eject, Eject, Eject. But who sits there and braces and gives the thumbs-up and hangs on as, once again, he's flung out to sea. Who's maybe OK while he's airborne and up there, flying the mission, on cruise control, enjoying the view, but feels sweat trickling down his ribs as the time comes to take his place in the recovery formation, who is so convinced that this time he's going to slam into the fantail that he comes in too high, misses all the arresting wires and bolts. Which means he's got to go round again, got to go round and come back and do the whole damn thing again which has become more difficult as a result of that earlier failure . . . If only, he thinks, he could be one of the guys on the deck, watching the planes come in, not doing it himself, just observing others doing it; not writing it, just reading about it.

36

For several days all the talk on board had been about the upcoming Steel Beach Party. The night before this much anticipated holiday I got back to find the usually empty corridor outside my room crowded and noisy with activity, with people—civilians. Their leader—fierce, bald, in his early sixties, still strong-looking—introduced himself as Harvey. He was from Texas and had masterminded the Steaks for Troops programme whereby God-knows-how-many tons of steak had been flown in, loaded aboard and would be served on the flight deck tomorrow by the folks milling around the corridor. That's who *they* were; but who, Harvey wanted to know, was this limey and what was he doing on board? (I am tempted to quote him as saying 'limey asshole' but I think this came slightly later in our exchange, and that, for the moment, limey was noun rather than adjective.) I told him about my time on the boat, how I'd been with a photographer who left yesterday.

'Better not try to take my picture,' said Harvey, 'or I'll rip your lips off.' I had become so accustomed to the extreme courtesy, consideration and politeness of everyone on board that I was somewhat taken aback by this threat. Not that I took it personally or entirely seriously; it seemed one only had to say something slightly out of line and Harvey would threaten to rip one's lips off. Twenty minutes after telling me he'd rip my lips off he told me how he'd told someone else he'd rip *their* lips off. His fondness for this aggressive turn of phrase in no way disbarred you from being in receipt of his considerable generosity and hospitality: long as you had your teeth you could eat his steaks with or without lips. So when he said I should join him and his crew for dinner I tagged along and found myself seated right next to him—an honour that the other people on his team seemed neither to begrudge nor envy.

I piled my plate in such a way as to make it look like it was piled up even though there was almost nothing on it—just the usual bits of pasta and a couple of dollops of lukewarm sauce. Harvey had made his money from burgers; the Steaks for Troops initiative was a way of giving something back. Before coming aboard the carrier he'd been on a cruiser, an experience which had made a great impression on him.

'I'm from Texas. We like *guns* in Texas. That cruiser's got some *big* guns. Bullet guns.'

'What, as opposed to ray guns, you mean?'

I enjoyed joshing with Harvey though the cut and thrust was diminished by the fact that he was deaf in one ear and that was the ear, naturally, that I was talking to. For top-quality banter you need sharp ears, you have to be an alert listener, and Harvey was somewhat hampered in that regard. He never smiled. There was just a lone-star twinkle in his hard-ass eyes, as he referred to me and those like me as 'media puke'. Over dinner, he told a long and complicated story about a black Air Force commander fucking someone's wife. Harvey had him followed by a former FBI agent and this agent slid the resulting file across a table in a diner to Harvey. The file included a photo showing this black officer taking the woman with whom he was having an affair into an abortion clinic. I wish I could have followed the story. It certainly seemed to touch on fundamentals—race, sex, betrayal, the rights of the unborn—but even after I had asked him to clarify certain details I could not untangle the ethical twists and turns. It occurred to me that we had not been bantering at all; or maybe only one of us had been—which meant that neither of us were.

37

I saw Harvey the next morning—the morning of the Steel Beach Party—in one of the walkways not far from our corridor. I had strayed from my normal route and was unable to find the Ward Room. He gave me directions but, as with his story over dinner, I couldn't follow what he was saying. I asked him to keep it simple because I was stupid.

'I hear you. Kiss,' he said. 'K-I-S-S: Keep It Short, Stupid.' He gave me the simplified version of where to go and then, before we parted, added: 'Don't eat too much cuz we gonna feed up your skinny little ass pretty good.'

Ensign Newell and I got up on deck at about ten thirty. The boat was completely still, as idle as a painted ship upon a painted ocean. So still I wondered if it was anchored. (Was that possible? Could the chain reach that far, all the way down to the oozy bed of the Arabian Gulf?) The planes were all parked down the front half of the boat. Tables and chairs were set out so that the deck—which looked way bigger than it did when flights were operating—was like the terrace of a seaside café. A sound system had been set up. A DJ was on the decks and on the deck, playing rock in the shadow of the island.

There were already a lot of folks up there, half of them out of uniform, in shorts and Ts, many of them queuing for steaks. Not that everybody had the day off. Strolling through the metallic tangle of parked F-18s I saw that quite a few jets were being worked on by mechanics, which made me wonder if, in the course of the day, I might bump into the bright-eyed woman from the hangar deck. Beyond the planes the very front of the deck was deserted. The ocean was a calm blue as if it had come out in solidarity with the ship, had declared today a no-wave day. Overnight the USS *George Bush* had become the best cruise ship in the world with a view of the sea unimpeded by guardrails—just angled nets to catch you should you wander over the side of the ship.

By the time I returned to the barbecue area the line of sailors waiting for steaks stretched right along the stern of the boat and for thirty yards along the starboard side. Paul and I got in line behind a woman wearing a pink USS *George Bush* T-shirt which, as long as you did not inspect it too closely, could have passed muster at a trance party. It didn't matter that we were in a queue; it was more like everyone was just conversing in linear formation. People who had finished queuing were sitting at tables and chowing down, or just sitting on the deck, chowing down. Everywhere you looked people were chowing down or waiting to chow down on Harvey's steaks. Nowhere else on the Arabian Gulf were so many people chowing down on such huge quantities of steak. When we got to the grills I could see Harvey himself, poking and rolling his steaks, not ripping anyone's lips off.

Paul and I found room at a table with a couple of his friends from the Reactor Room and an ordnance chief I'd not met before. He'd been in the Navy for fifteen years and, unprompted, offered up the simplest explanation as to why he—and almost anyone else—had joined up.

'Young enlisted or young officer, it was the best option we had at the time,' he said. 'For some people there's the pull of patriotism or a career but they're in a minority. For the rest it's just the best option at the time. That hasn't changed and won't change.'

Like everybody else he was tucking in to his steak with gusto while I just picked at mine, not chowing down on it at all. It was too obviously what it was: an undisguised lump of meat; there was nothing wrong with it other than that—and the fact, of course, that there was no beer to wash it down with. It was extraordinary, in a way, that there could be a party like this without a keg in sight, just bath-sized troughs filled with ice and soft drinks, Cokes and waters. The lack of booze meant that there was nothing here a militant Islamist could complain about—except, I suppose, women having a good time and wearing shorts. Maybe the music too. The DJ played a heavy country stomp and a whole bunch of sailors—black and white, men and women, in coveralls, uniforms or shorts—started *line dancing*. Oh, it was just tremendous. I asked a guy at the table what we were listening to.

'"Copperhead Road" by Steve Earle,' he said in astonishment, as though talking to the only person on the boat who didn't know this. I'd heard of Steve Earle but, somehow, had never listened to his music. And I'm glad I hadn't because there couldn't have been a better first time and place to hear this big-bellied hog-call of a song than here with these kids all lined up and kicking out their limbs as though the Gulf was just a big ole lake in a militarized patch of rural Texas.

Everyone piled their trash in cardboard boxes the size of kids' play pens. At the box for metals a young female rating collected the tabs in a box because they were made of a different, more valuable metal than the rest of the tin. It was like Burning Man again in the way that people always tried to pick up any bit of stay trash that was blowing about the place.

Spotting a brief lull in the queue for steaks I snapped a couple of prongs off my fork, broke my knife in two and went up to Harvey with my paper plate.

'Excuse me, Harvey, I wonder if you have any metal cutlery?'

'Why's that, limey?'

'Because my steak was so tough that it actually bust my fork.

And the knife too,' I said holding up the evidence. 'So I figure that if I'm going to get to make any inroads with all this meat I need some heavy-metal reinforcement.'

Before he had a chance to rip my lips off, I added: 'Just joking with you, Harv' and gave him a big smile. Unsure if he was in the market for jokes I walked quickly away and tossed my leftovers, plate and cutlery into the appropriate cardboard bins.

A football (American) appeared and was chucked around. Hip-hop was on the sound system. Racially I'd expected the day to be more . . . well, not segregated of course, and not like gangs in a jail, but more cliquey than it was. From where I was standing—next to one of the older crew members, stocky, late forties in grey T-shirt, shorts and a baseball cap, tucking in— it seemed like a model of racial integration. Oh, and that old- ish guy I was standing next to, I realized, was none other than Captain Luther! He had a lot on his plate—coleslaw, steak and bun—but I took this opportunity to ask about the party.

'If you help them create good memories they'll forget a lot of the bad stuff.'

'Well, you're creating a great memory for me today,' I said. I meant it too. The Captain told me about another great day—a day even greater than the routinely great days at sea—earlier in the deployment in the form of a Swim Call when everyone could jump off the side of the boat—or off one of the elevators at any rate—and splash around in the ocean.

'Tombstoning!' I said. 'I'd have loved that!' Obviously I'd have been more than a little self-conscious about being the skin- niest and second-oldest guy on the boat but I've always loved jumping into deep water from safe heights—does it count as tombstoning if you *know* the water is deep?—and I'm guessing they'd have checked to make sure there weren't any sharks in the vicinity before OKing the Swim Call in the first place.

'But tell me,' I asked the Captain. 'Where do you stand in the spectrum of naval commanders? I mean, are you progressive, forward-thinking, liberal—or more or less typical?' He didn't hesitate.

'I'm an old-fashioned forward thinker. Mission first, people always. We're on a warship so certain things have to be the way they are. But every sailor on this ship is a volunteer. They gave something up to be here. So we have to give 'em something back. A lot of it is just standard leadership. Eat after they eat, sleep after they sleep. Never give them an order if you don't understand what it'll mean they'll have to do.'

Not surprisingly, he didn't have much time or need for books on management—'We live leadership every day'—but he mentioned a story from a book called *The Seven Habits of Highly Effective People*. 'Two men in the forest are cutting trees. One keeps working all the time. The other takes a break every hour but at the end of each day he's always chopped more wood. The other guy asks him how he does it. Because every time I take a break, he says, I sharpen my axe.'

A football was flying through the air towards a lunging group near us. 'Better make sure that ball doesn't land on me,' the Captain called to one of the jumpers. I was curious to see what would happen if it did land in his coleslaw—but it never did and never would. Nobody was going to let that happen. They were chucking a football around but an axe was being sharpened. I thanked the Captain for his time and wandered off. It was the least I could do, a small courtesy: spare him the trouble of having to start a sentence with the words 'Well, I should be . . . '

Having wandered off I wandered straight back because 'Sweet Home Alabama' was on the sound system. This was destined to be one of the big hits of the afternoon—but it got mixed, halfway through, into another track so I wandered back to where I'd wandered back from. I bumped into Paul and together we spotted Admiral Tyson, also in shorts and T-shirt, down on the catwalk talking to a couple of guys playing guitar and banjo. Taking advantage of the fact that she was just hanging out, I asked about the pre-Navy days, when she was an English major. For some reason—my fault probably—the conversation turned to writers we didn't like.

'Well, I don't want to throw anybody under the bus,' she said. 'But I never really got on with James Joyce.' As in my previous meeting with her the admiral managed—that marvellous southern drawl of hers played a part—to convey a special warmth and intimacy to what she was saying so that a negative literary judgement seemed more like a reminiscence about that ole Jim Joyce, a somewhat eccentric neighbour whose fondness for puns, wordplay and telling everybody about his dreams had put an easily tolerated strain on everyone's patience.

After the admiral wandered off the guitar and banjo players played a duet, sweet and fast but dragging a railroad of sadness behind it. Paul and I spoke to them about a bluegrass band we all liked, the Steep Canyon Rangers from North Carolina. Then we wandered off also.

It really was like a festival, strolling round and coming across people doing their thing, some of them high-ranking members of the US Navy, some of them just chatting or playing music, and one of them completely on his own, in the sun, snoozing in a deck chair at the very front of the boat. He was like a lone figure in an Edward Hopper painting. I had no idea what he did on the ship but it's possible that he had a job that meant he rarely got to see the sea and sky. And whatever job he did it was certain that he never got silence—or space—like this to himself.

On our way back towards the island Paul introduced me to a tall, square-shouldered black guy dressed—incongruously on this holiday—in full uniform. He had a lot of medal ribbons on his chest, including—Paul explained—the Navy and Marine Corps Medal, awarded for saving a life.

'What did you do to get that?' I asked.

'We were driving home, my wife and I, and kids,' he said, standing at ease. 'Matter of fact, it was Thanksgiving Eve. There was a woman in a car alongside, unconscious at the wheel. She went into a diabetic coma. So I did what I guess you would call a cowboy move, a stunt-man move. Rammed the side of her car into the guardrail because she was unconscious and that was the only way to stop the car. I stopped the car, administered first aid to her, my wife called an ambulance and the rest is history.'

'Goodness me,' I said—an expression I hardly ever use.

'Yeah it was somethin'. But I do believe that any one of the individuals on this deck woulda did the same thing. In the position I was in I took the opportunity to say, "OK if it was my mother, my daughter or me I'd want someone to do the same thing."'

'And you got the medal.'

'Yeah I got the medal but the highest honour I got was the son saying thank you because that's the only mother I have. That was higher than any medal.'

My own mother had died four months earlier. That and the sure knowledge that I was talking to someone you could trust with your life made my voice catch in my throat when I said, 'Could you remind me of your name?'

'I'm Clinton Stonewall III, from Birmingham, Alabama.' Was it possible to cram more history into a name and a one-line answer?

'So where were you when they were playing "Sweet Home Alabama" just now?' I said, relieved to have something flippant to say.

'They were?'

'Well sort of. But they only played half of it.'

'That woulda made me upset because I'd have wanted to hear it all the way through.'

We had drifted over to the edge of the boat. Stonewall gestured at the ocean.

'Every morning when I get up I look at that water before we start flight ops. But that's the most amazing thing because water has a cycle, right? When it gets hot it evaporates, goes up to the sky, turns into a cloud, becomes precipitation and comes right back down again. You know that's the same water that Noah sailed on? That Christopher Columbus sailed on. And guess what? This day I'm sailing on that same water. I'm a part of that cycle. And you know we have a lot of technology up here. Man, this is the most powerfullest ship on the face of the earth. But that thing right there, that is power, it's beautiful, it's grace. And I'm inspired every time I see it.'

'And you know where those clouds end up?' I said. (I meant metaphorical ones; there was not a cloud in the sky.)

'Where?'

'England.'

'Ha ha. Right. I can be*lieve* that.'

The reason Stonewall was dressed so smartly, I discovered now, was not so that he could strut around showing off his kick-ass medal collection. No, later in the day he was being promoted and he hoped that I would come along to see the ceremony. I said I certainly would—but where was it being held? Taking advantage of the no-fly day, it would take place here on the flight deck, after the party which was already winding down. A lot of people had gone below deck. Tables, chairs and the remaining bits of trash were getting cleared away. Soon the big boxes of garbage would be taken away, the deck would be hosed down and everything would revert to normal.

The Steel Beach had become a flight deck—in nonflight mode—again by the time I went back up for Stonewall's ceremony. It was late afternoon, still light. Stonewall was standing in front of the island, being promoted from Lieutenant to Lieutenant Commander. A couple dozen people were there to witness the ceremony. One of these was the Captain, out of his shorts now, back in his flight suit. Stonewall's old ranking insignia were removed by two people and the new insignia secured by two others. Another ranking officer came up and read out the oath which Stonewall III repeated line by line. They met each other's eyes. After this Stonewall asked a friend to come up and say a prayer. When the prayer was over people asked Stonewall to say some words. The sky was ablaze with holiday light. A strong breeze was blowing. He stood there immense, smart and proud.

'I wanna say thanks to everybody for coming out, for finding time out of your busy day today. But this is not my day, it's your day. Look what you did. *Look what you did.* You put oak leaves on me. And I tell you now, I wanna thank each and every one of you, especially those who kept me upright and squared away. Thank you so very much. You know, I was reading the other night: on October 9, 1901, a young man was born into the world, name was Arleigh Burke, Admiral Arleigh Burke. He joined the Navy without a high school diploma. He'd had to drop out of high school and support his family because of the flu epidemic. But he still pursued his wish to join the Navy, he got a congressional appointment to get into the Navy—and the rest is history. I look at stuff like that. What if he'd said, "It is what it is"? A lot of people use those words as a token of giving up. What if he had said it? Forget about it. I'll just give up and look after my family. If he'd said, "It is what it is," then a lot of things we do today would have never been able to happen. What if the Wright brothers had said, "It is what it is"? We wouldn't have aircraft carriers, we wouldn't have aircraft to launch offa these things. I wake up and I go to sleep with this conviction every night, not to let it be what it is. I want to change, I want to *be* that change. And I thank each and every one of you.

'You know, it's not an AV clip here, it's camaraderie, it's the pride that we instil in each other and that pride goes a long way. I've been doing it now for twenty-one years and I tell you what, I thank each and every one of you. I love that shirt there, by the way,' he said, seeing the message stencilled on the yellow jersey of one of the guys in attendance: 'No weapon formed against us shall prosper.' '"*No* weapon formed against us shall prosper."' The guy wearing the jersey then turned his back so that Stonewall could read out loud what was written on the back: '"Believe that." Yeah, believe *that*! Because it's not business, ladies and gentleman, it's personal. You know that. I didn't put out to sea with five thousand business associates. I put out to sea with family members. And everything we do, whether it's up here on the flight deck, on the second deck or the seventh deck, I tell you right now, whether it's getting these catapults ready, serving in the meal line, whatever it is you're doing, it's all for me. You got my back. And I got yours. I tell you right now, Arleigh Burke was also quoted as saying, "Loyalty up and loyalty down." If you expect loyalty from your subordinates then you better show loyalty in return. Which means if you're a leader out here you need also to be a servant. The bottom's a reflection of the top. If you don't look good I don't look good. I think Vidal Sassoon had it right when he came out with that.' Stonewall had to pause here to let a wave of laughter die down. 'And if I'm looking good here today it's because of you. It's because of you.

'I look over at the statue of big George down in the hangar deck bay. This guy's geared up and in his flight suit. Don't know whether he's running *to* the battle or away *from* the battle but you know what? He's got a smile on his face. So be like good big George. Have a smile on your face. I don't care what happens in your day. Keep running and do it with a smile on your face. Thank you so very much.'

There was noisy applause but Stonewall was not quite finished.

'How you *feel*?' he boomed out.

'Good!' boomed back the reply from everybody there.

'HOW YOU FEEL?'

'GOOD!'

'HOW YOU FEEL?'

'*GOOD!*'

An understatement, to say the least. I felt so good—so *GOOD!*—I just wanted to stand there and sob. It was absolutely the most impressive speech that I had ever heard; to have quoted Sassoon (Vidal, not Siegfried) was a touch of genius. I also liked the seditious bit of sculptural analysis that acknowledged that big George might have been running away.* And to end the whole Henry-V-at-Agincourt bit of oratory with the injunction to keep a smile on one's face: a definitive rebuttal to the European objection that all the 'Have a nice day' stuff is just superficial.

People were lining up to shake hands, embrace Stonewall and pound him on the back. I shook his hand too but couldn't meet his eye because mine were full of tears. I thought back to what he'd said earlier, during the Steel Beach Party, about having only one mother. What would his mother have thought if she'd heard and seen him just now? Or his daughter? Impossible to imagine more love and more pride than they would have felt today. How many moments are there in a man's life to rival that?

I went back to my stateroom. What a day! The weather. The ocean. The view. The planes. The Steel Beach Party. The Steve Earle song. The line dancing. The Captain in his shorts, the Admiral in hers. Stonewall's promotion and speech. It was one of the great days of my life, and I could hardly believe the luck and privilege of being a part of it, even if only as an observer, an outsider.

---

* There was another statue of big George in the ship's little museum, together with a video about his time as a Navy pilot during the Second World War. On one occasion his aircraft was hit on a bombing raid and was immediately 'engulfed in flames'. He continued on to the target, dropped his bombs on the target and continued flying. By this time, the commentary explained, the flames were really bad (suggesting, at the risk of being slightly pedantic, that the plane had not been totally engulfed before). George instructed his two crewmates to bail out but managed to ditch the plane. He was rescued by a submarine. The two crew members died.

38

An unpleasant taxi driver in Albany, in upstate New York, once told me that my bad day had just got worse. Now, incredibly, my great day was about to get better.

At breakfast I'd eaten a few bananas, a bowl of cereal; later, I'd gnawed on one of Harvey's lumps of meat. In spite of what he'd said earlier Harvey had not fed up my skinny little ass good (though the fault, it could be argued, was mine). For dinner I'd had some tinned vegetables, cold pasta with tomato sauce and a couple of plums. After that, as an additional source of torment, I was going up to interview Captain Cook . . . Sorry, I mean the Captain's cook, CS2 Leesa Zilempe (Culinary Specialist Second Class). She had a nice little galley and it was easy to forget, up here, that she was in the Navy at all. It was more like she was a private chef on a yacht whose owner's taste in decoration was so austere as to be militaristic. Leesa had previous experience of journalists, had been displeased by an article which claimed she was making baked halibut when it was actually fried. I was going to have to be really on the ball here.

'I feel I have to say at the outset that facts are not my strong point,' I said. 'To be perfectly honest, strong points are not my strong point. But I'll do my best.'

Leesa's ambition was to cook at the White House. This was never going to be an easy ambition to fulfil but her determination to do so was another emphatic rejection of the it-is-what-it-is attitude to life. One of the reasons I am so bad with facts is that things are always reminding me of other things. In this instance, as soon as what she said reminded me of what Stonewall had said, I found myself thinking of my mum and dad who, for as long as I could remember, had impressed on me the importance of *accepting things*. It wasn't one's ability to change things that was important; it was one's capacity to put up with things, to suck them up. A direct product of their oppression, their lack of opportunity, this stoicism served them well, particularly my dad, especially in later life when he became burdened by all kinds of unchangeable and, one might have thought, unendurable hardships. So much so that, in his West Country way, he became a kind of personification of some Eastern ideal of nonresistance to life's vicissitudes. I, on the other hand, with the gradual expansion of opportunity afforded by grammar school and then Oxford, became conscious of an inability to accept anything. Far from being able to take things as they were I always wanted them to be different but lacked Stonewall's energetic (and very American) belief in the ability to make a difference.

I tuned back in to what Leesa was saying—though to put it like that is slightly misleading; I had scarcely even tuned in before I'd drifted off. It was while working at a restaurant where a benefit for Camp David was being organized that her desire to cook at the White House took hold. She had a mass of debts from culinary school; the Navy would pay off those debts and was, in addition, a natural stepping stone to the White House. And so, two days after the benefit, she joined the Navy.

For the first six months her job was cleaning, getting the galleys ready for action. She was in the Chief's Mess. When the actual cooking started she volunteered for everything. Volunteered for more and more. Work started at four thirty in the morning but she didn't wait for four thirty; she was determined to work at the White House so she'd get in at three thirty and work till eight in the evening. Her colleagues were expected to make two products a day; Leesa made eight and she made them from scratch ('because I wanted to work at the White House *so* bad'). She needed to get above everybody else and worked as hard as she could all day to do so. Then she got the watch-captain's job which meant, after the preparation and the cooking and the cleaning up, she had to do all the paperwork as well.

Even though I accept that ambition is, in certain circumstances, a good thing I have always disliked ambitious people. I have an allergic reaction to them. But standing here in the Captain's galley, leaning on the immaculately cleaned counter, I found myself not only liking Leesa, but rooting for her as though I were listening to the culinary equivalent of a *Rocky* film, a chef's version of Barack Obama's journey to the White House.

Except it didn't quite work out that way. The recruiter made a mistake or omitted to do something and the debt repayment to which she was entitled—and which was a major reason for joining up—never happened. By the time this was discovered, at boot camp, it was too late to do anything about it. Except (again), she discovered later (too late), there *had* been time to do something about it at boot camp but it would have required a lot more effort than the people at boot camp were willing to make. So she still had a ton of student loans and by the time she applied for the White House her debt-to-income ratio was too high. And yet her determination to cook at the White House was undimmed.

By now—by the time we met in her galley—Leesa's debt-to-income ratio was in better shape but there was another catch: you can only apply for the White House every three years so she'd have to re-enlist for another four. Which would make a total of nine years in the Navy.

It was a remarkable story and one which justified, in some serendipitous way, my unprofessional habit of drifting off and thinking of other things. Because now, after all that work, all those long hours of volunteering and dedication, she was going to have to accept things—exactly as my mum and dad always counselled. But how could she accept this? How could she not feel cheated, betrayed by oversights and incompetence—the very things that, as far as I had observed, were so common in civvy street but which the US Navy exhorted its members to eliminate? Especially since, she claimed, this kind of foul-up or oversight with regard to loans was not uncommon. The American paradigm of effort and energy rewarded had turned into a sad story that lacked even the vast and desolate consolation of tragedy. Had I detected something of this in Leesa from the outset? Was that why, contrary to my usual instinct, I had felt such warmth for an openly ambitious person who was so keen to get ahead? Had I seen that this was to be a story of ambition unrewarded and thwarted? If so, perhaps it was a necessary corrective to the gleaming professionalism—perfectionism even— that was such a feature of life on the boat. For all the talk of opportunity and the possibility of advancement the Navy is such a huge and monolithic institution that individuals are bound to get caught up in its regimens with almost no recourse to . . . well, to justice.

The decision of whether to re-enlist or jump ship was a source of torment for Leesa. She had three months to go. If she decided to get out then she would try to work in Paris, and then perhaps move back to San Francisco. I was so touched by the injustice of what had happened that I started saying something about Chez Panisse in Berkeley, California. Seeing Leesa's eyes light up at the mention of this famous restaurant I somewhat overtook myself and instead of saying that I knew someone who worked there, as one of Alice Waters's assistants, I claimed to know Alice herself (whom I had never met) and that I would do whatever I could to see if there were any openings there. It wasn't just boasting and name-dropping, though it was a little of both. I was still fired up by Stonewall's speech and wanted to do something to help, to watch her back, to stop things (it) being what they (it) were (is—or was).

After a somewhat delirious swirl in which a future job at Chez Panisse seemed not just possible but almost guaranteed we focused again on the here and now, on what the Captain wanted from his cook. 'Be creative and go crazy' were his words, which was great for Leesa. Especially since he was so *easy* to cook for. He liked good food.

'Who doesn't?' I said and the conversation turned to the poor quality of food available elsewhere on deck. I had trouble with that food, I said. Did she feel that if she was in charge she could do something to improve the quality of the food which I was having such trouble with, such *terrible* trouble. I did not look particularly pitiful as I said this, I had no ulterior motive in mind, I was definitely not trying to take advantage, in any way whatsoever, of the Chez Panisse carrot—the organic, locally grown, heirloom carrot—that I had dangled tantalizingly in front of Leesa a few minutes earlier; I was not angling for any kind of dinner invite, but the fact of the matter is that Leesa's next words were among the nicest I heard in the course of my stay on the boat, putting in the shade Stonewall's frankly overwrought oratory. These words were: 'Would you like some food?' The way the emphasis fell in her question—not 'would you like some *food*?' but 'would you *like* some food?', as if the idea of food had been introduced into the conversation by me and it was up to her to respond in any way she pleased as long as it was with reference to food—suggested that I maybe *had* been working some kind of angle, albeit unconsciously. Now that the cat was out of the bag I was fully conscious and felt no inhibitions about seizing the opportunity.

'Fuck, yeah!' I said, followed by a half-hearted and thoroughly implausible, 'if it's not too much trouble.' But what could be too much trouble—what difference did one extra dinner make—for someone who had worked fifteen hours a day in the hope that it would land her a job at the White House or Chez Panisse? And it really was no trouble, it seemed, as she set to work rehabilitating leftovers from this evening's dinner.

'It'll be seared chicken breast with grilled zucchini and a port wine reduction.'

'That sounds OK,' I said. 'Now tell me about the specials.' I was in a superb mood suddenly, a *gloating* mood as the galley filled with the clank of pans and the smell of lovely food being prepared for me alone. Yes, for me alone. Paul wasn't getting a look in. Not a taste. He had absolutely gorged himself on the crap they were serving down in that toilet they called the Ward Room. Ha ha! No wonder he stood there looking so down in the mouth, an expression that redoubled my anticipated pleasure.

While my dinner was being prepared I continued to ask Leesa whether she thought she could turn around the quality of food available for the boat as a whole but, to be honest, I wasn't really interested. All of my attention was focused on my meal and so, when it was served, was Paul's.

'Oh, man . . . ' he said, looking totally crushed, as I surveyed my plate.

'Remember what Stonewall said earlier,' I said. 'You watch my back . . . and I'll tuck in. Bon appétit, Ensign Newell.'

Although I tucked in I made sure I tucked in slowly. I moaned and went, 'Hmm, delicious' the whole time. And although I was joking about Paul not being able to eat any of it at some level my enjoyment was enhanced by what I saw—reverting to a word that had come to mind a few minutes earlier—as the simple *justice* of the situation. It was so obvious to me that I *deserved* this meal more than anyone else on the boat, that no one else had suffered from the bad food—the appalling food—as intensely as I had. And the Captain, I realized now, had been a little economical with the truth of his leadership principles. 'Eat after they have eaten' should have been followed by 'Eat way better than they ever could!' The chicken was tender and moist, and subtle and full of different flavours. I even crunched through a few bones but they felt tender too.

'That was amazing,' I said when I was done. It was as if Leesa and I had just finished having noisy sex and I'd rolled over, totally sated by the experience. There was even cake for dessert but I felt so stuffed I wrapped up half of it in a napkin and stashed it away for later. My shrunken belly was taut as a beachball. I thought of Stonewall and his great speech and how happy and proud he'd felt earlier in the day. I had my own room to sleep in and had just scarfed down a delicious meal made by the Captain's cook. I hadn't saved anyone's life or made a speech, but I'd made some wisecracks and I was happy with the meal I'd eaten and was feeling immensely pleased with myself and the way everything had worked out. Stonewall's doubtless was a higher kind of happiness, but his was not available to me, and mine, more to the point, was not available to him—and my belly was full to bursting with it.

And still this epic day had (a little) more to offer. The Captain had intended showing a movie up on deck, beneath the stars. That plan had to be abandoned: it had become too windy and the screen would have acted like a sail. A shame. I had no desire to see *Pirates of the Caribbean* part three—even more idiotic, presumably, than the first two in the series—but I would have enjoyed strolling round the starlit deck, watching people watching the movie. Instead, the movie was being shown in the hangar bay.

It was packed down there, with people on fold-up chairs or just sitting cross-legged on the floor, munching popcorn, cheering at the appropriate moments, gazing at the gigantic screen with its view of ships on a blue film of sea.

39

The next night Paul got in on the act too. He went up to Leesa's galley to see if any leftovers were available for me and came back to my room with a plate for himself as well. We both tucked in to these enormous portions of salmon and pasta. Yum. It was fantastic. It was tasty. It had flavours, it was tender. Paul had to leave as soon as we had finished tucking in and so, for dessert, I tucked in to the cake that I had squirreled away the night before. I was supposed to be here as some kind of reporter but I had ended up living like a castaway or hostage, a hostage who had been kidnapped by himself and was, as a consequence, developing a peculiarly intense and rare form of Stockhausen syndrome.

You see the state I was in? I meant *Stockholm* syndrome but maybe it was Stockhausen syndrome (whatever that is) that I was actually suffering from. I chortled to myself as I tucked in to my cake and felt my tummy growing taut as a beachball again, an even bigger beachball than it had been the previous day. I must let the world know what has happened to me, I said to myself, must write a message, seal it in a bottle and find a way of chucking the bottle overboard when no one is looking—especially the Captain. *Mayday,* it would read. *Jump the swimmer! I am Beachbelly, writer-in-residence aboard the USS* Stockhausen. *I am a hostage on the USS* Stockhausen. *I am the internationally renowned author of the* Helikopter Streichquartett *and a bloated bildungsroman called* Swimming the Jumper. The more I said USS *Stockhausen* and Beachbelly to myself the more I chortled and the happier I felt. That I found this incredibly funny may itself have been a classic symptom of Stockhausen syndrome, I said to myself as I sat there in my room, abundantly happy, bloated and chortling away like there was no tomorrow.

40

There really was almost no tomorrow—or only a couple of them, anyway. In two days I would be gone—and, as a result, I succumbed to my own version of the gate fever that begins afflicting the crew near the end of their deployment. I kept fearing that my name was not on the list for the Greyhound (it was; I checked twice), that the flight would be cancelled or that there would be an accident and it would crash with me on board (this last was the least of my fears; at least I would not be *inconvenienced*). I also worried—after the near loss of my exercise book on the flight in—that my baggage would somehow be mislaid. The details don't matter except insofar as (that phrase again!) they proved that I was desperate to get off the boat. I'd had one of the great experiences of my life, I wouldn't have missed it for the world—and I couldn't wait for it to be over with.

Yes, Beachbelly was bouncing back to the beach. Shore leave! Liberty! Freedom to explore the fleshpots of Bahrain! More exactly, the chance to use his Gmail account—from his hotel room. To eat proper food (less of an issue since he'd been gobbling leftovers from the Captain's kitchen) and drink beer. Beer! But did he even *want* beer? Hadn't he enjoyed the booze-less sleeps and the absence of the feeling of tipsiness and wooziness which usually signalled the day's sag into night? Would he in his small way miss the institutions of ship life he was so impatient to leave behind?

And it's not like I suddenly stopped enjoying being on the ship. Something was almost always being added to the apparently unchanging routine of the day. The whole of one morning was taken up with replenishment at sea (RAS). On the starboard side we were refuelled by a boat riding along next to us, umbilically joined by six pairs of hitched and drooping fuel lines. It was the equivalent not of pulling into a gas station but of having a gas station pull alongside you. Forced into straitened circumstances the ocean foamed and rushed between us like a white-water river. The other boat was battleship grey, as, I suppose, was ours—a shade of camouflage that seemed more effective in the Atlantic than here where sky and sea were always Arabian blue.

On the other side, in a far less intimate relationship, was another boat from which a helo flew back and forth, coming to us with a low-slung load of supplies, returning empty-handed. The trio of boats surged along together like this for an untold distance in finely calibrated—and extremely dangerous—harmony.

Even without exceptional events like this my life was more interesting than the one to which I would soon return. On my penultimate morning I went up to Vulture's Row to watch the surge and return of planes. One of the chiefs I'd had lunch with a couple of times was already up there.

'How ya doing?' he called out.

'I'm great, thanks,' I yelled back. 'How about you?'

'Sun's shining, wind's blowing, jets are flying,' he shouted back. 'Doesn't get much better than that!'

He was right—but it could so easily have been a lot worse than that. It had been tricky arranging dates that fitted in with both the Navy's logistics and my own surprisingly crowded diary. The first dates proposed were in late November, at the tail end of the deployment, when the carrier would be making its dismal way back across the Atlantic. I couldn't make those dates but I also pointed out that the weather, at that time of year, in the middle of the Atlantic, would be terrible and that I had been traumatized by the episode of *The World at War* devoted to the Battle of the Atlantic (the merchant convoys, the wolf packs). When this was relayed back up the chain of command the fact that I was *unable* to make the dates got deleted so that it seemed that all I cared about was the weather. I straightened this out: yes, of course I *preferred* nice weather to nasty but that was secondary to my other commitments and obligations—thank God! I realized now that it would have been not just unbelievably dreadful but completely pointless to have been on the carrier in the heaving and grey Atlantic in late November. No jets flying—i.e., the carrier might just as well have been a cargo ship—and weather so cold that the so-called flight deck would have been like an empty highway in the middle of the ocean. Rough seas and the crew counting down the days and minutes, waiting to get home with nothing really to do (though you can bet they were kept busy) in a state of steadily increasing boredom and impatience.

41

For his last evening Beachbelly would not be getting any left-overs from the Captain's cook. Because he would be back eating slop with the rest of the crew? No, because he was dining at the Captain's table. The Captain's in-port cabin—as it was bizarrely called—was modelled on a room in the Bush family home but with smaller windows (covered to prevent telltale light beaming out into the hostile night, the enemy night). The lighting was not soft but the furnishings were, the sofa was. Beachbelly sat on it somewhat stiffly, looking around. Lots of portraits of Bush and family looking midway between regal and regular, not troubled by the knowledge that, having chased Saddam out of Kuwait, they'd passed on the chance to settle his hash for good (thereby making a rod for their son's back). Maybe the pictures were taken before that, when their main worry was that this son of theirs was showing signs of being a bit of a retard.

There were seven guests for dinner, plus Captain Luther, who had not yet joined them. Beachbelly was the only civilian, but he was wearing a clean and pressed shirt that he'd kept in reserve for precisely an occasion such as this.

The Captain arrived in his flying suit as if he'd just flown in, business class, in an F-18. Everyone jumped up, including Beachbelly who stood for a few seconds in compromised at-ease attention until the Captain waved them all to table. Beachbelly was seated immediately to his right. He did not need to understand the exact significance of this to be conscious of the honour. To his right was someone he'd interviewed a few days earlier whose name he'd forgotten and whose rank he'd never understood (though he knew it was high). Beachbelly got the impression that this high-ranking neighbour was wondering why *his* unranked neighbour had spent the last two weeks wasting everyone's time.

The table was set with wine glasses, filled either with water or iced tea. The mere presence of these glasses initiated in Beachbelly a craving for wine more intense than any actual wine could have satisfied. Everything about the table and place settings cried out for a decanter of burgundy, but there was no decanter and there was no burgundy. It was like a vision of life after everyone had been twelve-stepped into sobriety and Beachbelly was the only one tormented by the knowledge that it didn't have to be this way, that there was a place for moderation, for staying up late, for opening another bottle and saying things like 'One for the road, anyone?' or 'Night cap, Cap'n?'

The food started to arrive and Beachbelly was not disappointed: Thai coconut soup, followed by crispy duck breast, mango chutney and perfectly cooked rice. Perhaps it was no better than the food he'd scrounged up the last couple of nights but there was a big difference between scoffing it like a stowaway and enjoying it here, as a legitimate guest at the Captain's table.

Just before joining the carrier Beachbelly had read Michael Ondaatje's novel *The Cat's Table* in which the narrator passes on 'a small lesson' learned in the long sea voyage from Ceylon to England. Contrasting the lowly status of the table where he dines every night with that of the captain's table where people were 'constantly toasting one another's significance', he insists that 'what is interesting and important happens mostly in secret, in places where there is no power. Nothing much of lasting value ever happens at the head table, held together by a familiar rhetoric.' Maybe so, but the food is certainly better which, at this point in the deployment, was all Beachbelly cared about.

And Ondaatje's point, he decided, was itself a form of rhetoric. It all depends on who's *at* the head table. Captain Luther had a permanent sparkle in his eye, could not have done more to put people at ease. He was the subject of a little respectful ribbing but he was, of course, the Captain so everyone was on their best behaviour which meant he had to do lots of the ribbing himself. The day before he'd completed a marathon on the treadmill—a good place to be, he claimed, since he was 'never more than a gurney away from a defibrillator'. Perhaps part of him longed *not* to be the Captain, for a relationship of complete equality where everyone is judged not by their rank but by the content and quality of their wisecracking. It was impossible to get a sense of him outside of his Captainness. But it was difficult to imagine his equivalent in the Royal Navy being any more charming or equable. Beachbelly wondered if it was acceptable to initiate a topic himself, was tempted at times to venture some conversational gambits but then thought better of it. What would it have been like to have dined with the Captain in Paris, where he was travelling after the ship docked in Marseilles on the way back to Virginia?

There was talk of baseball or football, none of which meant anything to the English Beachbelly. He didn't mind. He was, as they say, *savouring* his duck breast, savouring both its inherent duck-breastness and the fact that it was not whatever slop they were eating on the rest of the carrier. He looked up when he heard the Captain say, 'The event horizon of information. It goes there and stays there,' and wished he'd been listening to what had led up to this interesting remark rather than concentrating solely on his now-vanished duck breast. It too had passed over the event horizon.

The sparkle in the Captain's eyes could not conceal the impacted tiredness behind the sparkle. On a good night he got five hours sleep. That's what he'd been aiming for last night, setting his alarm for six thirty, but there'd been phone calls every half hour from about three thirty about ships approaching too close, stuff that, while not exactly urgent, required his authorization. Beachbelly could not have handled that. He was not a leader. He was Beachbelly and Beachbelly loved his sleep.

Dessert arrived—a chocolate thingy—and then everyone signed the menus and posed for pictures. Coffee and herbal teas were served, dinner was over—the Captain took a call on his radio—and everyone was trooping out, returning to their stations. It occurred to Beachbelly that he could have relaxed more than he had, but he remembered that, at the time, while they were at table, he'd judged it inappropriate to *appear* too relaxed. The main impression, though, was the sheer speed of the dinner. It had flashed by but rather than feeling short-changed he wondered if this was a model that could be adapted for use back on the beach. Invite people round for eight p.m. and send them off, full-bellied, by nine. It would never work—because of the ingredient so conspicuously missing from the Captain's dinner: alcohol, booze, wine . . . But how nice it was to get up from the table not feeling half asleep and semi-deflated, but bouncy as a ball, ready for Ensign Newell's promotion in the Flag Mess.

42

The Flag Mess filled up with more than a hundred sailors and airmen in flying suits, digital camouflage or coveralls. It was crowded vertically as well as horizontally: not everyone was my height, but the gap between heads and the low ceiling was conspicuously minimal. Paul was being promoted alongside another ensign and their part of the ceremony was to be followed by other awards for various outstanding performances. Admiral Tyson was making a short speech. I could barely see her above the sea of heads but she had no trouble making herself heard.

'This is a big deal in case you didn't know. We got two ensigns up here. One has been in the Navy for fourteen years and one's been in for eight years. Both of these guys started as E-3s in the Navy and here they are today being promoted to JGs [Lieutenants Junior Grade]. What that tells me—and I say this every time I get the opportunity so you might well be sick of it.'

I wasn't sick of it—I hadn't heard it before—but I had the feeling I'd had many times before on the boat, far more frequently than I had it in the normal course of civilian life, of intense liking for someone combined with intense admiration. A lovely combination that—and one that the admiral embodied: to be admirable *and* likeable.

'One of the things about the military is we all come in for whatever reason but it's a level playing field and you can make of it what you will. The opportunities are there to succeed and you can go as far you want to. So today we're gonna make 'em JGs and who knows how far they can go.'

Then, turning to Paul and his colleague, she said, 'I wish your family and friends were all here to see this, but we know we're your best friends anyway.'

In her down-home way the admiral was as impressive a speaker as Stonewall. The fact that she—an admiral—could speak in this homely style was actually one of the most impressive things about her. In her way she exemplified the achieved ideal of the level playing field on the occasionally pitching deck of a flat top.

I was glad that the last thing that happened during my time on the carrier was Paul's promotion. He was the person I knew best, the person I had spent the most time with, and he was so *deserving* of promotion: someone who incarnated all that was decent, reliable, dependable—and who was charming, funny and *so* easy to be around. The older I get the more I like that: being around people who are easy to be around. When I was told—by Newell—that I would be escorted round the ship by someone (usually him) my heart sank but I ended up feeling less at ease when he *wasn't* around. None of this, of course, can excuse the absurd moustache he'd continued to cultivate for the length of my visit; in a civilian institution that moustache would have been grounds not merely for passing him over when it came to promotions but for a dishonourable discharge.

Two people took off the gold bars on Newell's collars and replaced them with silver ones (so that the promotion seemed like a relegation or downgrading). The first of the returning jets came thumping down on the flight deck, drowning out Paul and his companion as they swore an oath to 'to defend the Constitution'.

After the ceremony was complete the admiral advised us of a potential change to the ship's schedule, which would not affect the planned date of return to the US—though the November weather could be relied on to do that. This bit was classified, the admiral said, so I felt somewhat conspicuous, standing there with a pen and notebook, jotting it all down. A couple of people looked me over, not suspiciously, just in an acknowledging-the-security-risk way. I tore the relevant page out of my exercise book, crumpled it one-handed and fed it into the nearest thing to a shredder I could find, namely my mouth.

43

On my final morning a woman called Angela came to change the sheets and prepare the room for the next guest. The place where I'd been sleeping in such privileged isolation could not have been more different from her berthing: she was sharing with more than fifty other women—though it didn't seem to worry her.

'I know how to share. I'm more adjustable than most. Instead of making them adjust to me I adjust to them so it's easier for me to commune. I prefer to have my own space, but I know how to make it comfortable so they don't have to worry about me and I don't have to worry about them.'

She was twenty-eight. Before joining the Navy she'd been a supervisor at UPS, and before taking care of the guest suites she'd been up on the flight deck.

'How was that?' I asked.

'We carried the chains, we dived and ducked, at night we washed the jets. We had to get the sea salt and sand off of 'em. Check the engine oil, check the level got good, check the tyre pressure.' She made the flight deck sound like a potentially dangerous garage back home in Chicago. Then she made it sound like something else, in rural Illinois: 'Flight deck, once you know it and know what to avoid, it's like being in a river.' She had the gentlest, sing-songiest voice I'd ever heard. Her voice was like a river and I could have listened to her for hours, just floating along, going with the flow of words, hearing her say, about the flight deck, 'It makes the time go by *fast*. When you're up on the flight deck time *flies*.'

Time was not flying for me. It had stalled. The minutes were anchor-heavy. I was eager to leave, to have done with noticing and remembering and trying to pay attention to complex explanations of things and processes I could not understand while worrying about banging my head the whole time. The fact that I was a volunteer did not diminish the tension of these last moments. It all came back to the first new word I'd heard: the trap. You're on the boat and you're trapped. Well, I was done with the trap and impatient for the cat. I wanted them to send me on my way to Bahrain, a place I had no desire to go to or see. I wanted to get back to my wife and my flat with its nice lighting and windows, its dimmer switches and quiet, where it did not sound, every couple of minutes, as though the roof over one's head was going to be rent asunder by forces so intense and clamorous they almost defied comprehension. I'm ready to go, I said to myself, ready to slip the surly bonds of earth, so put me in that bird, strap me in, and shoot her up.

44

I was ready to go, impatiently waiting for Paul, and so, for the last time, I resorted to the equivalent of calling him on the phone: I farted and, sure enough, like rubbing the lamp to make the genie appear, this brought him knocking on my door. For the last time we walked the hall of mirrors, through the knee-knockers and walkways that were busy, as always, with people cleaning, polishing and shining and standing aside to let us pass. At the ATO shack Paul and I said goodbye. No hugs or tears, just a handshake, eye to eye, man to man, Christian to atheist, sailor to civilian.

The ATO shack was already crowded with people waiting to fly out. Among them was a woman we'd lunched with occasionally, part of the group of young graduates who worked in the reactor. I didn't recognize her at first. She was wearing jeans and a blue T-shirt with something about Chicago on the front. I could see the shape of her breasts and her bare arms. Her hair was down—she had very long hair. Worried that if I sat anywhere near her I would not be able to keep my eyes off her I sat on the other row, facing away, facing the wall, thinking about what I'd seen and, more tormentingly, what I'd not seen. How effectively her uniform had concealed not just the body but the *womanliness* within. Even when they were exercising in T-shirts and shorts, I realized now, the women had none of the Lycra allure of gym classes in the city or the supple, quasi-erotic confidence and calm that one notices (without appearing to) when a bunch of women go to a café after a yoga session. No, they were just pounding along on the treadmills for all they were worth. The only sexual impulse I'd had—and it wasn't even remotely *sexual,* just a diluted form of romantic curiosity—had been concentrated on the woman from the hangar deck with the luminous eyes. And now I was suddenly conscious of that absence, of thoughts and feelings I'd not been having.

This is what was going through my fifty-three-year-old head in the ATO shack. What about the heads of the nineteen- and twenty-year-olds who'd been on deployment all these months? Was I the only male here exhibiting—i.e., taking pains not to exhibit—such lecherous thoughts? Perhaps their thoughts were more mature than mine. But how could they have been? Or maybe, in the course of the seven-month deployment, they had not been as oblivious as I had during my two weeks. What felt to me like a revelation after the fact, they perhaps had glimpsed, registered, understood and mentally stored away on many other occasions on the boat. In spite of all the rules governing displays of affection and so on there must have been a constant current of sexual attraction coursing through the ship the whole time. Perhaps this belated 'lechery' of mine was a symptom of diminished sexual feeling, an inability to pick up on something which, despite the asexualizing uniforms and codes of behaviour was, to the youth of the boat, unmissable and omnipresent.

I did not have to sit for long in the ATO shack, staring at the wall. Soon—cranials on, vizors down—we began trooping up to that other world, the flight deck, in single file. Black-vizored faces and colour-coordinated jerseys directed us to the waiting Greyhound.

Sky. Ocean. Silence. Wind blowing. Jets moving and parking. Just the same—just as amazing—as on any other day. Time flying.

Another great day at sea.

On the plane we strapped ourselves into our seats. However I adjusted them the buckles of the shoulder straps were directly over my collar bones. The safety briefing had emphasized the intensity of the forces—the negative G—that would be unleashed when we took off. Our seats were facing backwards so we would be flung forward, against the straps. I signalled to the naval air crewman (as I now knew the flight attendant should be called).

'What's up, sir?' he yelled.

'The buckles are digging into my collar bones.' Even though I was yelling it still sounded feeble.

'What do you want me to do about it, sir?' he yelled back again. If it had been a little quieter and if I had been feeling less anxious I might have replied, 'I'd be obliged if you could adjust them so that I can sit more comfortably. And when you've done that perhaps you'd be so kind as to bring me a gin and tonic with ice and a slice of lemon.' Instead, I shouted out my very real fears.

'I'm worried that when we take off I'm going to break both my collar bones.'

He grinned. 'Not gonna happen, sir.'

Then what would happen, given the alarmist nature of the safety briefing? What happened was that we sat there for another ten minutes, during which time I continued adjusting all available straps and wriggling in such a way that the buckles were slightly above my collar bones. As a consequence the waist strap was no longer around my waist but over my lowest ribs so that they were at risk of splintering as well. Finally, when I was sure the propellers were increasing in volume prior to take-off I pulled all the straps so tight I could hardly breathe. I crossed my hands over my chest as I had been told, I looked down to make sure that my feet were on the bar in front (also as instructed) only to discover that there was no bar. The engines roared more loudly. The flight attendant gestured to indicate that we were about to go.

The take-off was like nothing I had ever experienced—with the emphasis on nothing. A further roar of propellers. A jolt forward—no real sense of momentum, the faintest addition of pressure on the collar bone—and then part of the carrier went blurring past the window and we were low over the water. Airborne! We were not ploughing into the sea. We had left the carrier and were laboriously clambering up steep stairs of sky. People began taking off their cranials, loosening straps that were already a lot looser than mine. I followed suit, did what they tell you to do on a commercial aircraft: I sat back (figuratively speaking; I was still bolt upright), I relaxed, I enjoyed the nothing-happeningness of the flight.

The drama of take-off did not make sense until we landed in Bahrain. We descended so gradually that only the occasional pressure on the ears gave any sense of what was happening. The wheels hit the runway and we sped along for what felt like a couple of miles before slowing down, stopping.

We were back at the beach.

45

In two short weeks I had become thoroughly habituated to life on the boat. This too became apparent only when I was back on the very dry land of Bahrain. I checked in at the hotel, went up to my room and showered for a long time. The shower was super-luxurious, a source of pleasure, not merely a way of getting clean as quickly as possible. The water itself felt cleaner, more sparkling. I washed my hair using palmfuls of shampoo and conditioner, dried myself with a fluffy white towel the size of a flag and dug out unworn clothes from my suitcase.

I hadn't realized, while on board, how dirty everything was. My shoes looked like I'd been working in a garage, my exercise books like they'd been scrawled in by a guy with learning difficulties at the front desk of a place that employed fifty mechanics. My little Dictaphone and camera were greasy. Everything, even if it wasn't actually greasy, was coated in a thin suggestion of oil. The only time my laptop had left my stateroom was when it was taken onto the Greyhound; I had always washed my hands before using it—but the keyboard seemed smudged and oily. The fuel and grease of the gigantic workshop and airstrip that is the carrier had seeped in everywhere. This is not surprising; the surprising thing was that I'd not noticed it on the boat.

I looked out of the window at the empty cityscape that is Bahrain and experienced another revelation: I could go for a walk!

For the purposes of tourism Bahrain is right down there with the least interesting places on earth. People on the carrier who'd spent time in Bahrain said the best thing to do was just watch a movie in my room but the freedom to walk around, in the open air, was amazing.

It was Eid, a public holiday. The roads were deserted. Everywhere was so empty and quiet it was difficult to tell the difference between the vast tower blocks that were not yet ready for occupancy and those that were already functioning as high-rise dwellings. The fact that it was a holiday, that there were so few people around, made the contrast with the crowded life of the ship more marked than if I'd disembarked in London or New York, enhancing the extraordinary fact that there were streets instead of corridors. These streets were sky-high and, relatively speaking, desert-wide. You could walk without stooping, could cross the roads without wearing a cranial. You didn't even need ear protection.

There was no sign of the political unrest that had made it seem possible that the Arab Spring might have spread here by the autumn. There was no sign of anything really, just Indians or Bangladeshis who were in Bahrain to work, walking in little groups of three, and a few tourists—American, I guessed—enjoying one of the benefits of travel afforded by the Navy: the opportunity to visit a place that is not worth visiting. But they were, I suspect, enjoying exactly the same sensations that I was, relishing the opportunity to walk, to go where you pleased. I was hoping for nods of recognition, some sense that we were part of the same tribe, but I was not shaven-headed and well-muscled: I just looked like a scrawny expat, a leftover from a novel Graham Greene had decided not to write. It was blazing hot and, while it may have been humid, the air felt dry as old toast. There was nothing to see.

I went back to my room and watched a football match—English football, real football: Spurs versus Fulham. Now that *was* worth seeing! Later I had dinner in the hotel restaurant: a Thai green chicken curry which, relative to almost everything I'd eaten on the boat, was sensational but which compared poorly with the Thai meal I'd eaten the night before, at the Captain's

table. I had a beer with dinner and made sure I looked at it, all
golden and cold and sweating before I tasted it. It tasted like . . .
well, like beer. It was OK. It wasn't the beer of my dreams, the
Ice Cold in Alex beer I'd been longing for. It was just Heineken.
Maybe it would have been different if it had been Sierra Nevada
or a crisp pilsner. I had no desire for a second glass.

After dinner I saw a couple of thickset, shaven-headed guys
in T-shirts, shorts and flip-flops who looked military. They were
waiting for the elevator with a couple of women in dresses and
heels who looked prostitution. I waited for the next elevator and
returned to the absolute silence of my hotel room, the silence
which served as an amplifier for noise, though this only became
apparent later on, after I'd turned out the light. A fire door connected my room to the one next door, through which came the
excited sounds of . . . not, thankfully, of humans having sex but
of a man alone, like me, watching the game on TV. An American man living the thrills and disappointments of a football
game (American) just as I'd done a few hours before. Relative
to the boat it was as quiet as the grave in my room—but it was a
grave from which I was exhumed every few minutes by shrieks,
whoops, cries of encouragement and groans of disappointment.
I turned on the bedside light and called him on the phone. He
was watching his home team, he said, and hadn't been aware of
all the hollering he was doing. He was nice as pie, as nice as Jax.
I didn't hear a peep from him again.

I'd kept my curtains open so that I could see the city at night,
an uninteresting extent of buildings, lights and, beyond that, the
unseen sea. It was almost ten o'clock. On the carrier there would
soon be the little announcement and prayer that preceded Lights
Out. I thought of my stateroom and wondered what little story
was being told tonight over the Main Circuit before the prayer.
How lovely it was to end the day that way, to hear the words
'Let us pray . . . ', to hear some final and gentle version of the

thing that was emphasized throughout the day by anyone and everyone: do better, excel, work to the best to your abilities, for yourself and everyone else.

Exporting my routine from boat to hotel, I turned off my bedside light and lay in the massively luxurious bed, remembering bits of psalms and hymns that I'd always liked, passages about those in peril on the sea, those who go down to the sea in ships and do business on the great waters. There was an acknowledgment in such lines that there is something especially vulnerable about the vocation of the sailor out there, as Stonewall had said, on the same sea as Noah.

What does it mean to pray? How can you pray if there is nothing to pray *to*? I don't know. I thought of Paul bowing his head over his plate as if asking the Lord for the power to get this slop down his throat without puking. You wouldn't catch me doing that—I'd rather go without until I found a way of getting my hands on leftovers from the Captain's table.

I didn't pray when either of my parents were dying or after they were dead. I just sucked it up until, after a time, it didn't feel like sucking something up; it just felt like life, like life underwritten by a constant suggestion of death.

Prayer is an ability and habit that has gone away, atrophied—unless it means something very simple, like thinking of people, thinking fondly of them, wanting the best for them, hoping they come to no harm. If that counts, then that is what I did; I prayed for those who go to the sea in ships.

Appendix: US Naval Rankings

TITLE	ABBREVIATION	PAY GRADE
Seaman Recruit	SR	E-1
Seaman Apprentice	SA	E-2
Seaman	SN	E-3
Petty Officer Third Class	PO3	E-4
Petty Officer Second Class	PO2	E-5
Petty Officer First Class	PO1	E-6
Chief Petty Officer	CPO	E-7
Senior Chief Petty Officer	SCPO	E-8
Master Chief Petty Officer	MCPO	E-9
Fleet/Command Master Chief Petty Officer	FLTCM/FORCM	E-9
Master Chief Petty Officer of the Navy	MCPON	E-9 (Special)
Warrant Officer 1 (no longer in use)	WO1	W-1
Chief Warrant Officer 2	CWO2	W-2
Chief Warrant Officer 3	CWO3	W-3
Chief Warrant Officer 4	CWO4	W-4
Chief Warrant Officer 5	CWO5	W-5
Ensign	ENS	O-1
Lieutenant Junior Grade	LTJG	O-2

Lieutenant	LT	O-3
Lieutenant Commander	LCDR	O-4
Commander	CDR	O-5
Captain	CAPT	O-6
Rear Admiral Lower Half	RDML	O-7
Rear Admiral Upper Half	RADM	O-8
Vice Admiral	VADM	O-9
Admiral Chief of Naval Operations/Commandant of the Coast Guard	ADM	O-10
Fleet Admiral (reserved for wartime)	FADM	O-11 (Special)
Admiral of the Navy (retired rank)	AN	

Acknowledgments

I am grateful to Alain de Botton who first asked if there was somewhere interesting I would like to reside and write about, and to Caro Llewellyn at Writers in Residence who made it happen so easily (well, easily for me, at any rate).

Ongoing thanks to everyone at the Wylie Agency, especially Andrew, Sarah Chalfant, Kristina Moore, Luke Ingram and Davara Bennett.

Thanks to Chris Steele-Perkins, the snapper, for his marvellous photographs.

My biggest thanks, obviously, go to the crew of the USS *George H.W. Bush* for the unflagging friendliness, good humour, professionalism and patience extended to me throughout my stay. Their patience needs emphasizing: it must have been difficult to accept that a simple technical explanation of a fairly straightforward process would have to be repeated three or four times—and still be greeted with the blankest of blank looks. I spoke to a lot more people than are featured in this book and I would like to thank all of them for taking the time out of their already crowded schedules. As is obvious from the text, Paul Newell has to be singled out for special praise and thanks. He was a wonderful guide and friend; it was a great privilege to witness his promotion at the end of my stay and I wish him every success and happiness in his career and home life.

As will by now be clear there are times in the book when I take issue with opinions expressed by certain crew members. This in no way diminishes either my respect and gratitude for their willingness to speak openly to me or my admiration for the dedication and enthusiasm they bring to their work. Needless to say, all mistakes are mine alone.

This book was made possible by a grant from Writers in Residence, an association devoted to placing some of the best writers and Magnum photographers in some of the key institutions of the modern world. Writers in Residence seeks to bolster the long-form nonfiction essay and the art of photojournalism.

For more information, see *www.writersinresidence.org*.

Founder: Alain de Botton
Editorial Director: Caro Llewellyn

Other Writers in Residence books include:
Liaquat Ahamed and Eli Reed: *The International Monetary Fund*
Douglas Coupland and Olivia Arthur: *Kitten Clone: The History of the Future of Bell Labs*

A NOTE ON THE TYPE

This book was set in Granjon, a type named in compliment to Robert Granjon, a type cutter and printer active in Antwerp, Lyons, Rome, and Paris from 1523 to 1590. Granjon, the boldest and most original designer of his time, was one of the first to practice the trade of typefounder apart from that of printer.

Linotype Granjon was designed by George W. Jones, who based his drawings on a face used by Claude Garamond (ca. 1480–1561) in his beautiful French books. Granjon more closely resembles Garamond's own type than do any of the various modern faces that bear his name.

Designed by M. Kristen Bearse